LETTING THE TEXT WIN

DR. J.K. JONES

DR. MARK SCOTT

Joplin, Missouri • 1.800.289.3300 • www.collegepress.com

Copyright © 2014 College Press Publishing Company

On the web at www.collegepress.com
Toll-free order line 1-800-289-3300

Printed and Bound in the
United States of America
All Rights Reserved

Designer: Mandie Tepe

ISBN #: 978-0-89900-494-5

FOREWORD

Twenty five years ago I relocated to a new ministry which afforded me the rarest of opportunities: a chance to sit under the teaching of the authors of this book. As a young preacher, I was still looking for my voice and wanted to get better at my calling, so I audited a course offered by Drs. Jones and Scott entitled "Advanced Biblical Preaching." I was seeking guidance from some experienced preachers for what I was thinking at the time. Young preachers like me often think that advanced preaching means discovering some new revelation, insight, or "secret sauce" that will improve their sermon effectiveness: "Perhaps the key to great preaching is learning to tell stories better." "Maybe if I could just increase my proficiency in the Bible languages my sermons would have depth." "If only I could figure out how to bring fresh insights to old verses." "How can I be more in touch with the culture and people I'm preaching to in order to make my teaching relevant?" Maybe you can relate.

Too often these thoughts can become the preacher's focus. The unfortunate casualty is that the more advanced preachers become in their craft the more they exclude the written word they intend to proclaim. Many times as the preacher gets better at identifying and telling stories, understanding complex theology, and exegeting the culture; he is tempted to relegate the Bible to proof texts, authoritative punctuation marks, and spiritual decorations for the sermon.

What I learned as a young preacher a quarter of a century ago, you will happily learn with me again in this writing. Advanced biblical preaching is about the Bible! We don't need more creative preachers, eloquent preachers, brilliant preachers, or relevant preachers. We need preachers who will begin in the text, pray in the text, live in the text, and speak the text into our context. This book by my professors and now good friends will help us in our journey to become these kind of preachers—preachers who let the text win.

MIKE BAKER
Lead Preacher
Eastview Christian Church
Normal, Illinois

my thoughts than my thoughts.

10 "For as the rain and the snow come down from heaven, and return not thither but water the earth, making it bring forth and sprout, giving seed to the sower and bread to the eater, shall my word be that goes forth from my mouth; it shall not return to me empty, it shall accomplish that which I purpose, and prosper in the thing for which I sent it.

you shall go out in joy, and be led forth in peace; the mountains and the hills before you shall break forth into singing, and the trees of the field shall clap their hands. the thorn sh

CONTENTS

FOREWORD – Mike Baker 3

INTRODUCTION – JK 7

CHAPTER 1
Letting the Text Win – JK 11

CHAPTER 2
Letting the Text Win: An Historical Survey – MS. 25

CHAPTER 3
Letting the Text Win Over the Preacher – JK. .41

CHAPTER 4
Letting the Text Win in the Study: Part 1 – JK .53

CHAPTER 5
Letting the Text Win in the Study: Part 2 – MS 67

CHAPTER 6
Letting the Text Win in a Sentence – JK 95

CHAPTER 7
Letting the Text Win over the Sermon's Sequence – MS 105

CHAPTER 8
Letting the Text Win over the Illustrations – JK. 119

CHAPTER 9
Letting the Text Win over the Imagery of the Sermon – MS 131

CHAPTER 10
Letting the Text Win in the Beginning and the End – JK. 145

CHAPTER 11
Letting the Text Win in the Worship Service – MS 157

CONCLUSION – JK 167

APPENDIX A
Tips for Letting the Text Win in a Postmodern World – MS 169

APPENDIX B
How to Know If the Text Is Winning – MS 171

APPENDIX C
Two-year Sample Sermon Series Plan – JK 173

WORKS CITED 183

my thoughts than my thoughts.

10 "For as the rain and the snow come down from heaven, and return not thither but water the earth, making it bring forth and sprout, giving seed to the sower and bread to the eater, shall my word be that goes forth from my mouth; it shall not return to me empty, shall accomplish that which purpose, prosper in the thing for which sent it.

shall go out in joy, led forth in peace; tains and the hills before reak forth into singing, he trees of the field shall eir hands. he thorn sh

INTRODUCTION (JK)

Mark and I love to preach. We offer this confession with great delight. God, in His oceans of grace, has called us and blessed us to carry out His commission. Our fathers, Bob Scott and John K. Jones Sr., modeled it for us and we dedicate this book to them. Our teachers, people like Don DeWelt at Ozark Christian College, John Webb at Lincoln Christian University and Dr. Wayne Shaw at Lincoln Christian Seminary, have immensely influenced our preaching. Now we find ourselves in their place as teachers of preaching and encouragers of preachers. This book is presented with a spirit of deep gratitude to our heavenly Father and to all those He has used to impact and shape our lives. J.K. would particularly like to express thanks for the editing help of Alan Kline, former registrar at Lincoln Christian University. He is deeply appreciative of the invaluable input of Josh Bennett, preacher, brother in Christ, and former teaching assistant; the wisdom and encouragement of Mike Baker, preaching minister, cherished friend and partner in eternal Kingdom work at Eastview Christian Church, Normal, Illinois; and the insight and contribution of Dr. Chuck Sackett, Professor at Large, Lincoln Christian University, preaching minister at Madison Park Christian Church, Quincy, Illinois, and most importantly, friend and brother in Christ. Thank you. Thank you. Thank you.

> The primary motivation behind the writing of this book was to join our voices together and... elevate the importance of the biblical text winning...

Several years ago College Press asked if we might consider writing a textbook on preaching. We prayed, pondered, and finally accepted the invitation. We realize that the field of preaching is loaded with many excellent resources. Perhaps you are asking, "Why another textbook on preaching?" We asked that question ourselves. The primary motivation behind the writing of this book was to join our voices together and write a book on preaching that attempted to elevate the importance of the biblical text winning over the various aspects of the preaching task. We also acknowledge that the joy of working on this project together lured us. We have been close friends for years, and our families have been just as close for several decades. We studied together in seminary. We have taught together in the past. We have traveled together, eaten lots of meals together, prayed together, shared hotel rooms, stayed in each other's homes, played together, laughed together and even cried together. There is a oneness of spirit and heart that we hope saturates the pages of this book.

> ...a picture of preaching as a great relay of truth. We want to help you to have some sense of your place in that glorious race.

Letting the Text Win is intentionally designed to help the new and inexperienced preacher capture a methodology in sermon-making, as well as discover a theology of preaching that he can build on for a lifetime. Please do not feel the need to read the book from cover to cover. We highly encourage you to pick and choose those chapters that scratch your biggest itch. Consider your own preaching. Where do you really want to grow? What part of your preaching needs some improvement or refinement? Give concentration to the chapters that speak to your current need.

The book also seeks to address some of the needs of the more experienced preacher. We hope *Letting the Text Win* will be an encouraging reminder of the size and scope of this great undertaking and a kind of refresher course to those who have been doing this for a while. We want you to have the best experience possible. Therefore, this brief synopsis of the book is given. Chapter one describes what letting the text win might look like and how that picture challenges the contemporary cultural context. Ultimately, the first chapter attempts to show how God is the primary communicator in the preaching event and how the preacher can best partner with our eternally articulate Creator. Chapter two paints a picture of preaching as a great relay of truth. We want to help you to have some sense of your place in that glorious race. Chapter three looks at some of the key biblical passages and terms that are essential for understanding the urgency and importance of preaching. These passages and terms help shape the interior world of the preacher and ultimately win his heart for a lifetime of proclamation. Chapters four and five focus on the way in which the biblical text

> We humbly pray that this book will bring glory to God through... letting the biblical text win.

must win over the study life and habits of the preacher. We will discuss methodology, hermeneutical principles, and the importance of genre awareness. Chapter six will deal with that elusive and challenging task of crafting the sermon in a sentence. If the text is going to win, then it must always guide and direct the dominant thought of that particular message. Chapter seven highlights how the text can win over the sermon's structure, skeleton, and movement. Chapter eight will suggest some tips for finding that elusive illustration and how the text itself can help you with that difficult challenge. The ninth chapter will coach the reader to let the text win over the imagery of the sermon, especially as it relates to painting word pictures, finding images, metaphors and similes that fit the message. The tenth chapter seeks to address the issue of sermonic introductions and conclusions. How do we let the text win over the opening and closing of our sermons? The last chapter tackles the larger context of letting the text win in the worship service through specific issues like pulpit posture, etiquette, style, and attention to the worship hour. We humbly pray that this book will bring glory to God through preaching and preachers marked with a reverence for and commitment to letting the biblical text win.

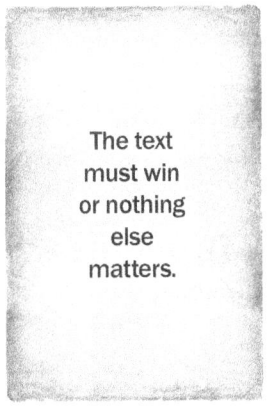

The text must win or nothing else matters.

The history of preaching is fascinating and mysterious. Those who have said, "Yes" to this great relay of truth have discovered that it is an oral event, not just a written one. Oral communication is at the very heart of all that takes place in proclamation. Some of us have noticed that in the early years of preaching the emphasis was upon saying what the biblical text said. The passage was taken seriously. Something changed, though, in the subsequent years. Preachers were taught to take their listeners seriously, so we spent a great deal of time studying and exegeting our audience. Now, at the opening of the 21st century, we are bombarded with voices that remind us of the importance of the manner and method in which we preach. We are taught to take the medium seriously. Experiencing the text has become paramount. All three of these reminders are vital, yet it seems to us that nothing else has significance if the first one does not have the priority in our preaching. The text must win or nothing else matters.

The reader will notice that the book is dominated with masculine talk. We acknowledge the limitation of the English language to convey all that we intend. Neither author believes that females cannot preach or teach. What exactly that may look like in a specific congregation is a debate and subject for another book. Both of us have taught homiletics and expository preaching to females. Perhaps the simplest way to express our heart is simply to quote George Barna in *Leaders on Leadership*.

> Unfortunately, our language does not have an inclusive pronoun, one that means "he or she." Consequently, we are left with several inadequate choices in sentence construction. The constant use of "he or she" is structurally cumbersome and often undermines the flow of the content. To insert "their" is grammatically improper. Thus, throughout the book we have utilized "he" as the primary pronoun related to the (preacher), solely to facilitate a smoother flow. (15)

The reader will also notice that Mark is a footnote-man, while I am a parenthetical-man. We trust this difference will not get in the way of a seamless reading of the book.

Dr. Clive Calver, past president of World Relief, tells of visiting an African village in the Sudan. Dr. Calver saw 250 Africans gathered under the shade of a tree. He had been to Africa enough to know what that meant—namely, a worship service. He asked them what they were doing. Someone responded, "We're worshiping Jesus." Dr. Calver said, "You're worshiping Jesus?" "Yes," they said, "Do you know Jesus?" Dr. Calver replied, "Yes, I know Jesus." The Africans responded, "We heard there is a book." "Yes, there is a book," Dr. Calver assured them. The Africans replied with great curiosity, "Have you seen this book?" "Yes," he said, "I have several copies of the book back home." The Africans were totally amazed! Then Dr. Calver said, "Look, the church in America brought you seeds to plant, so you can grow food and your children won't die." The Africans said, "Oh, that's nice. Please tell the people in America, thanks for the seeds. But could we have the book first?" Could we have the book first? There is the question! The focus of *Letting the Text Win* is to help the preacher restore the primary place of that Book!

"...thanks for the seeds. But could we have the book first?"

CHAPTER 1
LETTING THE TEXT WIN (JK)

"Dusty Bibles lead to dirty lives." I first heard those words from the late Dr. Howard Hendricks, gifted teacher and much-loved professor of Christian Education at Dallas Theological Seminary. I don't know if they are original with him. It doesn't matter. That sentence has been permanently stored away in the hard-drive of my soul. For me, they radically emphasize the importance and urgency of Scripture. They also remind me that the Word of God is intended to speak to my everyday life. God preaches to me when I open up His Word and listen to His friendly voice. Simply put, Christian preachers seek to say what God is already saying. Authentic Christian preaching desires for the text to win by finding the message of the sermon in the meaning of the passage. Dusty Bibles not only lead to dirty lives, but they lead to sloppy preaching and shallow preachers.

> Dusty Bibles not only lead to dirty lives, but they lead to sloppy preaching and shallow preachers.

I deeply appreciate the perspective of Bryan Chappell. "The ethic of expository preaching is plain. Because we believe that the power of spiritual transformation resides in the Word of God, the goal of the preacher is to say what God says" (*Preaching Magazine*, September–October 2004, 9). The shout of this book is, "Let the biblical text win over your preaching!" The whisper of this book is, "Let the biblical text win over your life."

Almost immediately, some of us begin to call up memorized passages of Scripture that speak of the priority and power of the Word of God. We think of Genesis 1:3, "And God said. . . ." All creation breaks loose as His word brings into existence land, sea, light, living creatures, and ultimately man and woman. Some of us run to Joshua 1:8 and recall the challenge and promise offered to a leader feeling rather lonely after the death of Moses. "Do not let this Book of the Law depart from your mouth; meditate on it day and night, so that you may be careful to do everything written in it. Then you will be prosperous and successful."

> It is like watching the sun awaken and stretch its arms of morning colors across the sky!

A few of us recall our own desert experiences in ministry and we quote Jeremiah's words when the weight of preaching God's prophetic word was overwhelming him like a tsunami. "When your words came, I ate them: they were my joy and my heart's delight . . ." (15:16). There are even those of us reading this book who would choose to repeat his later words, "But if I say, 'I will not mention Him or speak any more in His name,' His word is in my heart like a fire, a fire shut up in my bones. I am weary of holding it in; indeed, I cannot" (20:9). Even if we are not familiar with Old Testament Scripture, and this whole preaching business is new to us, we might have come upon Isaiah's memorable words.

> As the rain and snow come down from heaven, and do not return to it without watering the earth and making it bud and flourish, so that it yields seed for the sower and bread for the eater, so is my word that goes out from my mouth: It will not return to me empty, but will accomplish what I desire and achieve the purpose for which I sent it. (55:10-11)

Personally, I absolutely love to find my theology of Scripture and God's communicative power in the Psalms. My poet's heart delights in hearing the many contributors offer their unique voice in praise to God's Word. I am drawn to the high view of the author of Psalm 19. It is like watching the sun awaken and stretch its arms of morning colors across the sky! When I read these words I see the grand horizon of the biblical text.

> Investigate the vastness of Psalm 119 like you were Meriwether Lewis or William Clark.

> The law of the LORD is perfect, reviving the soul. The statutes of the LORD are trustworthy, making wise the simple. The precepts of the LORD are right, giving joy to the heart. The commands of the LORD are radiant, giving light to the eyes. The fear of the LORD is pure, enduring forever. The ordinances of the Lord are sure and altogether righteous. They are

more precious than gold, than much pure gold, they are sweeter than honey, than honey from the comb. By them is your servant warned; in keeping them there is great reward" (19:7-11)

Who among us, after reading Psalm 119, doesn't have this great passion to spend the rest of our lives in living a Word-honoring life? I would encourage any preacher to periodically journey through this longest chapter in Scripture with an explorer's heart and mind. Be a biblical Christopher Columbus or Ernest Shackleton. Investigate the vastness of Psalm 119 like you were Meriwether Lewis or William Clark. Walk around the text as if you were John Muir exploring the California Sierras. Take some notes while you read. Notice the energetic and vigorous language the writer uses to describe what God's Word is like. Study the way he imaginatively and creatively takes those eight primary words for Scripture and weaves them into a beautifully ordered, magically symmetrical, and wonderfully oceanic picture of the written word of God. Wow! What a great God! What an unparalleled communicator!

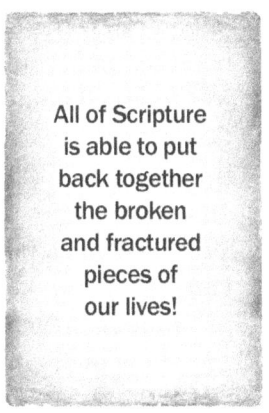

All of Scripture is able to put back together the broken and fractured pieces of our lives!

Of course, there are so many other passages that we could quote. The second part of our Christian Bible, the New Testament, continues the elevation of God's Word. Many of us quickly think of 2 Timothy 3:16-17. We rehearse in our minds that God Himself breathed out Scripture. Specifically the Old Testament Scriptures find their origin in God. That is exactly what the seasoned preacher, Paul, told Timothy, his young partner in ministry. Paul says that God made Scripture incredibly useful for teaching the truth, exposing sin and rebellion, redirecting mistake-filled lives, and coaching people to live in a way that pleases God. If these four objectives can be paired together, then right belief and right living are the primary purposes of Scripture. All of Scripture is able to put back together the broken and fractured pieces of our lives! Hallelujah! The writer of Hebrews adds this eloquent sentence to our discussion. I like how Eugene Peterson puts it. "God means what He says, what He says goes. His powerful Word is sharp as a surgeon's scalpel, cutting through everything, whether doubt or defense, laying us open to listen and obey. Nothing and no one is impervious to God's Word. We can't get away from it—no matter what" (*The Message*, Heb 4:12). Amen.

Consider some of the marvelous statements Paul makes about the Word and God's communicative power. ". . . How can they hear without someone preaching to them?" (Rom 10:14). "For the message of the cross is foolishness to those who are perishing, but to us who are being saved it is the power of God" (1 Cor 1:18). "My message and my preaching were not with wise and persuasive words, but with a demonstration of the Spirit's power, so that your faith might not rest on men's wisdom, but on God's power" (1 Cor 2:4-5). "And we also thank God continually because, when you received the Word of God, which you heard from us, you accepted it not as the word of men, but as it actually is, the Word of God, which is at work in you who believe" (1 Thess 2:13). "God's Word is not chained" (2 Tim 2:9). "Preach the Word" (2 Tim 4:2). On and on the Scriptures bear testimony to the impact of God's Word. Passage after passage elevates the supremacy of God's unequaled revelation of Himself. We can know Him because He first makes it possible. He is the preeminent preacher!

There was a time in the life and witness of a local church when talk of letting the text win or being a Word-directed congregation would have been assumed. However, since the dawning of postmodernism and the "truth is relative" philosophy, there has been an awakening among some Jesus followers to state more clearly the importance of Scripture. The Word of God is the authoritative and sufficient foundation. Crawford Loritts offers this reminder. "Inherent in preaching is a sense of divine authority that distinguishes it from merely good communication. Great preachers are good communicators, but good communicators are not necessarily great preachers. And the difference is authority" ("Preaching That Raises Our Sights" in *The Art and Craft of Biblical Preaching*, 36). So how does a teacher/preacher communicate God's truth in an age that has all but abandoned the notion of absolute truth? The answer to that question actually prepares the way for responding to the gigantic focus of this book: What does it mean to let the text win? It is my conviction that communicating God's truth in an age of relativism requires the preacher to be biblical, clear, engaging, creative, visual, practical, prepared, relational,

> "Great preachers are good communicators, but good communicators are not necessarily great preachers."

purposeful, and authentic (Michael Duduit, *Preaching Truth in a Whatever World*, November 2004). Consider that first characteristic: biblical. In one way I am talking about expository preaching and in another way, I am talking about something much, much bigger and grander. To let the text win goes far beyond a Sunday morning sermon. It implies an attitude of life or worldview. "What we truly believe determines what we do. What we believe in our heart of hearts about preaching will determine how we carry it out. In that sense, nothing can be more practical than our theology of preaching" (Jay Adams, "Theology of Powerful Preaching" in *The Art and Craft of Biblical Preaching*, 33). This conviction about preaching includes my own devotional life, my theological reflection, my study habits, my sermon preparation, my hermeneutical understanding, and my homiletical approach. Actually, it would be accurate to say that letting the text win or practicing true exposition of Scripture is more of an "attitude than a method. It is the honest answer to the questions, 'Do I subject my thought to Scriptures, or do I subject the Scriptures to my thought?' " (*Preaching to a Shifting Culture*, ed. Scott Gibson, 2004, 82).

> To let the text win goes far beyond a Sunday morning sermon. It implies an attitude of life or worldview.

Simply put, letting the text win is delivering a message from God that emerges out of the biblical text, in contrast to topical or thematic preaching, in which the major focus or tenet of the sermon emerges out of the preacher's own creativity and imagination. This book is not opposed to thematic or topical preaching, even though it seems to lean more toward opinion rather than exposition. Haddon Robinson warns us,

> When preachers announce a text they sometimes practice sleight of mind—now you see it, now you don't. The passage and the sermon may be nothing more than strangers passing in the pulpit. Yet, it is a rape of the pulpit to ignore or avoid in the sermon what the passage teaches. Topical preaching common in American pulpits flirts with heresy. (*Making a Difference in Preaching*, 70)

Thematic preaching can have a legitimate place in Christian proclamation. The caution here is that regularly preaching thematically can become just like Mark Twain's assessment of the Platte River: "An inch deep and a mile wide." I am calling for a kind of preaching where a biblical text drives the sermon. I don't mean that letting the text win is a line-by-line commentary on the biblical passage. What I mean is, the sermonic sentence the preacher settles upon, from thorough study of the passage, guides and pushes the sermon along. Allow me to repeat myself. This sentence is drawn from muscular study. It is accurate to the text, relevant to the congregation, and contemporary in application. We'll talk more about that later in chapters five and six.

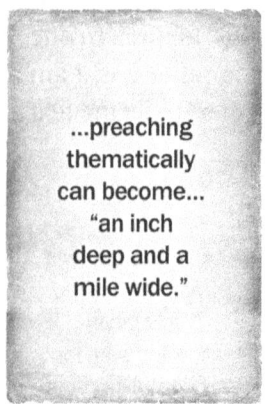

...preaching thematically can become... "an inch deep and a mile wide."

Not everything that can be said about a biblical passage gets into the sermon of a Word-led preacher. A preacher and congregation that are seeking to let the text win are praying and thinking about the text until that passage masters them, dominates them, sets their imagination on fire, and causes them to want to live under the authority of God's Word. The sermon is rooted in and shaped by the biblical text. I like the succinct way Jeffrey Arthurs defines preaching. Preaching is "accurately heralding the Word of God to a particular audience for a particular purpose by explaining, applying, and embodying that message" (*Preaching with Variety*, 15). Many of you reading this book know this heartbreaking truth: every church drinks from the deadly poison of the culture. A preacher and congregation that want the text to win recognize this and regularly consume the antidote of biblical preaching and biblical living. They both realize that what is needed in the twenty-first century is the unquestionable love and uncompromising voice of God. So, how does that happen week after week in the local church? There are, at least, three possible answers.

1. Listen to the Scriptures.

First, someone must be the lead listener of Scripture in the church. There must be, of course, lots of listening and listeners, but someone must set the pace. That someone is the preacher/teacher or the preaching/teaching team. You are a pioneer in this task. Roger Van Harn, a number of years ago, said, "Preachers are pioneer listeners on behalf of the community of faith" ("The Preacher as Listener," *Preaching Magazine*, Jan-Feb 1993, 2). This

...what is needed in the twenty-first century is the unquestionable love and uncompromising voice of God.

image calls for several applications. One concrete application is that the preacher/teacher takes the necessary time to listen to the Word. Many of my students are so eager to be relevant that they often work harder at being creative and imaginative, than actually studying the biblical text. They fail to take the needed time. This time factor is expressed at multiple levels. It can be evidenced devotionally when the preacher spends unhurried time contemplating and praying over the passage. The preachers that have impacted my life the most are those that have cultivated large interior worlds. They have taken the time to build strong and muscular devotional lives. That same time element can be seen systematically when the preacher reads through the Bible regularly and often. At this level he repeatedly reminds himself of the big picture and the details that make up that grand mural. My friend and dear brother in Christ, Dr. Bob Lowery of Lincoln Christian Seminary, kept this as one of his holy habits. He faithfully read through the Bible multiple times each year. The cumulative effect of this discipline is immeasurable. Of course, this time factor is also vividly seen in the studious heart of the preacher and teacher. The one who longs to be God's conduit must dig deep wells in the Word. I'm talking about a kind of spirit that resembles Ezra. The Bible says that Ezra "had devoted himself to the study and observance of the Law of the LORD, and to teaching its decrees and laws in Israel" (Ezra 7:10). He took great care to inquire of God and then do what God asked of him. The vocabulary suggests he did this continually.

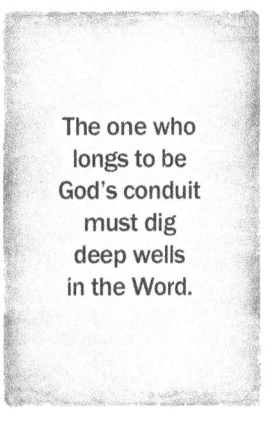

The one who longs to be God's conduit must dig deep wells in the Word.

The preacher who wants the text to win stays long enough in that text to clearly hear what God has on His heart. I love the old acrostic that reminds me of the time needed to accurately hear. I hope it will encourage and challenge you.

> **H**ours: invest the time, get a study schedule and stick to it.
> **E**ffort: discipline yourself. God in His grace has given you a spirit of discipline.
> **A**lertness: rest and take care of your body and mind so you can hear Him.
> **R**epetition: find a methodology that suits you in getting into and out of the text.

For some time now I have been fascinated by the stories that come out of the Oklahoma land runs. There were five runs in all from 1889 to1895. Some two hundred and fifty thousand people participated in those five runs. Anybody could run: women, former slaves, immigrants, the poor. I've seen actual film footage of some of those extraordinary races! It was not uncommon for people to be killed in the first 100 meters. Some were killed over disagreements on the property they claimed now belonged to them. It was dangerous business. The saddest part of the story for me is the way in which some tried to hurry the process. There were those who cheated! A few people snuck out early and posted their sign of ownership. They staked their claim that this particular piece of ground now belonged to them. These dishonest folks were labeled "sooners." If you followed the rules you were called a "boomer." To be called a "sooner" was incredibly derogatory! Like a sooner, a preacher can cheat too! A preacher who creates a sermon before really listening and studying the passage is a sooner. God's spokesman needs to listen patiently and attentively to the biblical text. He must hear the truth in order to tell the truth!

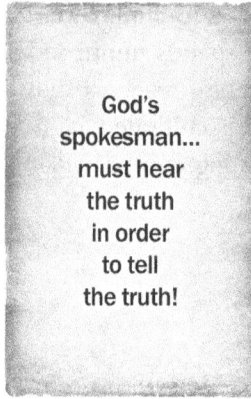

God's spokesman... must hear the truth in order to tell the truth!

2. *Listen to the Congregation*

Second, someone in that local congregation must regularly listen to the people who listen to him. Remember that much of the New Testament is a response in letter form from Paul, a preacher who listened to local congregations. You are a pastor in this task. I do not mean that you are the chief executive officer in that place. You are not the only pastor, but nonetheless you are a care giver, a shepherd of God's flock. Fred Craddock is right, "Study and preparation involve careful listening to the congregation, as well as the text" (*Preaching*, 39). John Stott has been a distant mentor of mine through his fine writings. In his classic work, *Between Two Worlds*, he wrote, "It is often and rightly said that the best preachers are always good pastors, for they know the needs and problems, doubts, fears, and hopes of their people. A conscientious pastor can never preach 'regardless of his hearers' requirements" (216-217).

This great challenge of listening to the congregation also encourages multiple applications for the communicator of God's truth. It means that we must pay careful attention to the ordinary. We must grow in our ability to enter the sacred world of small talk. God is present in those routine, everyday conversations in your study, over the phone, at the local café, and on the street corner. Preachers are like spies. We seek to discover what is latent and hidden. It requires a childlike curiosity matched by adult concentration. This listening business invites us to eavesdrop into holy places that seem rather unholy.

Perhaps an example will help you to grasp what I am attempting to say. I was a young preacher making a visit to one of the elderly women in the church. We had entered into the world of small talk over a cup of afternoon coffee and cookies. I had heard this woman's story a number of times. I knew it so well, or so I thought. She rehearsed for me how she had been abandoned by her husband and left to raise her two children alone. She described with great color how difficult those early years were. Then something unexpected happened. A mysterious and unannounced page of her story suddenly appeared. It caught her completely off guard. She began to slowly and painfully reveal a scene in the drama of her own narrative that she had never disclosed. One night when the weight of life was so oppressive that she couldn't take it any longer my friend decided to end it all. She told the children that they were going for an evening car ride through the country. When they had fallen asleep, she drove the car back to the house, pulled down the garage door, and waited for the inevitable. Somewhere in that darkest hour she became aware that God was present and whispering to her, "I'm with you. I'll see you through this difficult time. Trust me." Her profound transparency was punctuated with a flood of tears, hers and mine. We simply sat there quietly and prayerfully for a while. The sacred had invaded that afternoon visit. It struck me powerfully then and does even now. We never know when God will break through the everyday, routine conversations.

It requires a childlike curiosity matched by adult concentration.

If we are to really listen to the congregation, we must avoid the temptation to manipulate every conversation. It is so easy to control and police what people say to us. Good communicators cultivate conversational humility. They watch for the battles people face between grace and sin.

They remember that we are not hired just to do "religious jobs."

In my first preaching ministry I would walk from the parsonage down the street to the home of a woman who had been the victim of seven strokes. Her body was wracked with paralysis, and her speech was barely understandable. A daughter lived with her and cared for her. Each Sunday morning before Sunday school and worship I would make the short trek to that woman's house in order to pray with her, read Scripture, and share the Lord's Supper. Her daughter would place the bread and cup on her lips, and I would stand there in holy silence. That beautiful sister in Christ taught me how to listen for more than words, to listen beyond words. As I would go out the door, she would speak those same broken words, Sunday after Sunday, week after week: "I appreciate you." I would offer a feeble, "Thank you." I can still hear her weakened voice and still recall my feeling that I was taking an advanced course in shepherding and listening. Please don't miss this: the preacher who has ears to hear gives better sermons!

> Good communicators cultivate conversational humility.

Again, how does the preacher week after week grow in letting the text win over his heart and the heart of the congregation? There is a third answer.

3. Listen to the Culture.

Preachers are physicians in this task. How strange it is that we live in a culture that violently seeks authority, while viciously spurning authority. What a paradox! Scott Gibson's warning is sobering and challenging. "What has happened is that the authority for ethical decision making has become my story, my journey, my experiences, and my feelings. . . . Even the church has drunk culture's deadly poison" (*Preaching to a Shifting Culture*, 218-219). Many have undertaken the huge task of trying to help us understand the contemporary culture. In North America we are blessed to have resources that help us in preaching to a postmodern world. Of course, not every culture around the world is postmodern. The point is clear, however, that wherever you find yourself, if you are a communicator of the gospel it is imperative that you listen to the culture. Even a simple reading of Acts and the letters of the New Testament would reveal how those early preaching missionaries understood this.

The premiere example, of course, is Paul in Athens (Acts 17:16-34). He knew how to build the needed bridge between the truth of the gospel and the worldview of those who gathered there at the marketplace and the Areopagus.

Over the years I have constantly taught my students that when we listen to the culture we must remind ourselves of what we say we believe about Scripture. I list some of those reminders below.

1. The Word is a dynamic changing power (Isaiah 55). I can't say I let the text win if I don't spend enormous time in it.

2. The Word can accomplish everything that needs to be accomplished. I can't say I let the text win if I am constantly complaining about my own inabilities to preach and teach.

3. God identifies His name and reputation with the power of the Word. Haddon Robinson says, "If people can be exposed to an understanding of the Scriptures on a regular basis, then they do not need arguments about the veracity of Scripture" ("Convictions of Biblical Preaching" in *The Art and Craft of Biblical Preaching*, 23). I am not letting the text win if I am preoccupied with what people think about my sermon. What I want them to think about is God!

4. I must study, but it is the Holy Spirit that transforms the listener, not me. I'm not letting the text win if I think I am the change agent.

5. I must remember that God speaks through the public reading and preaching of His Word. I am not allowing the text to win if I do not prioritize the preparation and practice of reading my text and reviewing my message. I have been so blessed in my teaching experience to have partnered with several of the very best preaching professors: Dr. Wayne Shaw, Dr. Chuck Sackett, Dr L.C. Sutton, and Dr. Jeff Snell at Lincoln Christian University and Seminary and my partner in the writing of this book, Dr. Mark Scott. All five of these men are superb models of practicing the

> ...we live in a culture that violently seeks authority, while viciously spurning authority. What a paradox!

public reading of Scripture. All you have to do is hear these dear brothers read their own text aloud, and you get this great sense that they have practiced and practiced and practiced.

6. I must model the priority of Scripture in my own life. If the text is to win, it must begin by winning over me. I must make room for the text to talk to me. Alistair Begg is right, "The first heart God's Word needs to reach is that of the preacher. There will be no benefit to our people from expository preaching unless we ourselves are being impacted by the Scripture we are preparing to preach. It is imperative, when we are dealing with the biblical text, that we are personally changed by it" (*Preaching for God's Glory*, 34). Integrity and character compel me to come to the Word regularly and often with a spirit of humility and hunger.

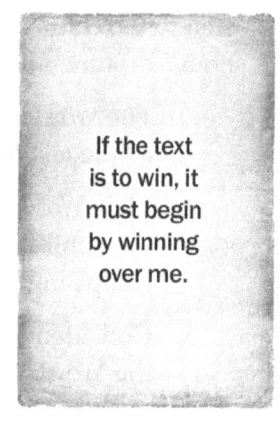

If the text is to win, it must begin by winning over me.

7. I must place my confidence in Scripture, not in my own gifts and abilities. The preacher that lets the text win is the preacher that has the highest confidence in the Word, or perhaps it is better to say, has the utmost confidence in the author of that Word. There is always a danger of slipping into professional "god-talk." In ways that I cannot calculate, Eugene Peterson has been a source of profound help and guidance over the years. In one of his masterpieces, *Tell It Slant*, he offers this introductory gem.

> Language—given to us to glorify God, to receive the revelation of God, to witness to the truth of God, to offer praise to God—is constantly at risk. Too often the living Word is desiccated into propositional cadavers, then sorted into exegetical specimens in bottles of formaldehyde. We end up with god-talk.... My concern is that we use God's gift of language in consonance with the God who speaks. (1)

As I grow older, I find that I am less confident in myself and more confident in the One who spoke His Word into existence.

8. I must remember that only the Word can meet needs at the deepest level. The text wins when I remember that truth. How many of us have been surprised by joy and amazed by grace as we watch Scripture minister to the hearts and minds of our listeners?

9. Because the Word comes to me in various forms, I would be wise to imitate that in my preaching. If I only preach one way, I am probably not letting the text win. Very few of us enjoy dining on the same meal day after day. We enjoy variety. What is true of our physical appetite is true of our spiritual hunger.

What I am trying to say is this: the preacher who listens to the patient (the culture) won't be guilty of malpractice. An intentional and Spirit-driven listening must be recovered.

I am a faithful reader of Scripture. It has taken years to get to the place where I daily practice the discipline of *lectio divina*, reading with God in mind. I know there are those who care as much about preaching as I do but who would think of me as naïve for putting so much emphasis on letting the biblical text win. Some would say that talking about the authority of Scripture is archaic and out of step with contemporary understanding of proclamation. They would suggest that the important thing is to allow the listener to simply "experience" the text. I am not opposed to emphasizing the need for our listeners to experience the biblical passage. There must be, however, something of greater size. My simple mind does what I have trained it to do—it runs to a passage of Scripture. "Above all, you must understand that no prophecy of Scripture came about by the prophet's own interpretation. For prophecy never had its origin in the will of man, but men spoke from God as they were carried along by the Holy Spirit" (2 Pet 1:20-21). I pray I will be like one of those ancient preachers who believed that the grass withers and the flowers fade, but the Word of the Lord stands forever. Now there's something with size!

> We enjoy variety. What is true of our physical appetite is true of our spiritual hunger.

I have long been fascinated by the story of the code-talkers of World War II. The United States Army looked for a way to transmit messages in Europe and the South Pacific without the Germans and Japanese being able to break

> We enjoy variety. What is true of our physical appetite is true of our spiritual hunger.

the code. They decided to use the Comanche and Navajo Indian tribes to pass along these life saving messages. Recently, the last code talker died. His name was Charles Chibitty, a Comanche who served in Europe. Before he died he said something that touched me deeply. "It's strange, but growing up as a child I was forbidden to speak my native language at school. . . . Later my country asked me to. My language helped win the war . . ." (*The Pantagraph*, 7/22/05, A13). If there ever was a need for biblical code talkers to speak their native language, it is now. We find ourselves in a great global spiritual war. The stakes have never been higher. Let the text win!

CHAPTER 2
LETTING THE TEXT WIN: AN HISTORICAL SURVEY (MS)

"What's past is prologue."[1] That is true of most things, but it is certainly true of the history of preaching. Preaching did not arrive where it is today without many influences. It is beyond the scope of this book to trace all of those influences. But we want to trace some of the more important historical developments[2] where the text won—or did not win.

The message of the history of preaching is that the text, when handled well, has always won. Albert Mohler said, "From the birth of the New Testament church until today, every significant phase of authentic revival, reformation, missionary expansion, or robust church growth has also been an era of *biblical preaching*.[3] Historically speaking, when the text wins, the congregation wins. When the text wins, the lost win. When the text wins, society wins. When the text wins, God wins.

The Word and the Words

We must begin this historical sketch with a theology of the Word of God. A proper theology of preaching will help us critique when the text has won in history. A starting point for a theology of preaching will actually take us back before Genesis 1. Before God's first words (Gen 1:3), there was the Word (John 1:1).

An age-old question is, "Which came first, the Bible or the church?" Our Catholic friends say, "The church." Therefore the church can dictate

---
1. William Shakespeare, *The Tempest*, act II, scene 1, lines 253-254. Antonio is speaking.
2. The author admits that this historical survey is quite limited. It mainly traces developments in the more recent Evangelical Christian West. Chapters could be added, by those more capable, on the influences of letting the text win from the Eastern Orthodox Church, the Western Roman Catholic Tradition, African and African-American preaching, Asian preaching, Latin and South American preaching, and the preaching from islands of the Pacific. At various points of history in all of these traditions the text has wins and losses. It should also be admitted that, given the cultural, geographical, and ecclesiastical constraints, some preaching in these traditions might be closer to the style of preaching evident in the New Testament than much preaching in the Evangelical Christian West today.
3. R. Albert Mohler, Jr., *He Is Not Silent: Preaching in a Postmodern World* (Chicago: Moody, 2008) 11. This quote actually is from the Foreword, written by John MacArthur.

what the text means because church people wrote the Bible. There is some truth to that assertion especially in regard to the New Testament. The forty human writers of the Bible were all insiders, that is, they wrote from a posture of faith. Our Protestant friends say, "The Bible came first." It stands above the church in authority. It may have been produced by inspired *insiders*, but it critiques even those who wrote it (1 Cor 14:37; Gal 1:8). Church architecture makes this abundantly clear.[4]

Without sounding too arrogant, we suggest that both groups are wrong. Neither the Bible nor the church came first. What came first was the Word. It predates the Bible. God came first. Jesus came first. The gospel came first (at least as far as the New Testament is concerned). The Word produced both the Bible and the church. It is important that we understand all the nuances of the phrase of "Word of God."[5]

> Historically speaking, when the text wins, the congregation wins. When the text wins, the lost win.

God acted and/or spoke before anything was written down. Long before Moses recorded the creation account, God created the world. Sometime before Moses gave Israel the Ten Commandments, God delivered his people out of Egyptian bondage. Before any of the Gospel writers took up a pen to give us the good news, Jesus was born, was raised, ministered, died, and rose again. In other words the historic *word* (God's activity) took place before anything was written. This will be a large claim, but we suggest that *preaching* actually lies behind much (if not most) of the Bible—the written word. John Stott says, "For Christianity is, in its very essence, a religion of the Word of God."[6]

Here is the further truth. When God's revelation of Himself did move from orality (and we could say aurality)[7] to the written word, it was written down in such a way as to be spoken again. That is why it is so very proper to "speak from the Bible." The Bible from its genesis is a speaking

---

4. In a Protestant Church the pulpit always sits above the communion table. How can one come to the table of the Lord if one does not know what it means?
5. Myron Taylor attempted this in his address to the college-career session of the North American Christian Convention in Detroit in 1977. His message was entitled, "Trust the Word." He nuanced six senses of the phrase, "Word of God," (eternal, historic, spoken, written, word of proclamation, indwelling). Myron Taylor, "Trust the Word," *The Christian Standard* (4 December 1977) 4-6.
6. John R. W.Stott, *Between Two Worlds: The Art of Preaching in the Twentieth Century* (Grand Rapids: Eerdmans, 1982) 15.
7. Much work has been done in the last two decades concerning the orality that lies behind the written text. Scholars understand much more about how an oral culture morphed into a written culture. In terms of preaching, see Bruce Shields, *From the Housetops* (St. Louis: Chalice, 2000).

book. This is why John Stott says that the Bible speaks now from what it already spoke then. The preacher comes to the text recognizing that, to some extent, the passage has already been shaped by the biblical writer, who was first a preacher. Orality is the primal reality that both predated and produced the Scriptures.[8]

A legitimate question is, "To what extent is the preacher's word the Word of God?" The Reformer's famous dictum was, "The preaching of the Word of God is the Word of God." While that statement exalts the pulpit, it may say more than the Bible itself permits. The Bible, the written Word, is objective. The canon sets the perimeters for that objectivity. There are sixty-six authorized books—no more, no less. Therefore the preacher always knows which words are his and which words are actually God's. The preacher's prayer is that through all his or her words will come the Word (see Titus 1:3; 1 Pet 4:11).

So, does God have a contemporary voice at all? We would respond with a resounding "yes." But, in what way? Some suggest that God speaks to them all the time. It is as if these people have a hot line from heaven. God tells them what shirt to buy, what book to read, and what gum to chew. What God seems to tell them has little or nothing to do with the Bible. On the other hand, some people suggest that God quit speaking when the New Testament was completed. He used to talk, but He has stopped now.

Is there a middle ground? Is there a way to recognize God's contemporary voice and maintain a fidelity to the Bible as God's primary voice? John Stott helps us with his work on Hebrews 3–4 and its use of Psalm 95.[9] The Holy Spirit "says" is present tense (Heb 3:7). But the quote is from Psalm 95. Stott says we can see four successive stages in which God spoke and speaks: first in the time of testing of Israel in the wilderness, secondly in the psalmist's use of that time of testing, thirdly in the Hebrew writer's context, and finally when the reader reads it today. The point of all of this is that God's contemporary voice speaks through what he has already spoken. The Spirit takes the written Word and gives it a fresh hearing for today. A hermeneutical presupposition is that a text cannot mean what it never meant. However this is not to say that

---

8. The progression would be something like this: God himself as Word, God's voice (creation), God's activity (Israel delivered from Egypt), God's book (OT), Jesus as Word, Jesus' activity (humanity delivered from sin), Jesus' disciples' word (preaching of the apostles), Jesus' book (NT), Jesus' book proclaimed ("memoirs of the apostles" is what Justin Martyr called it), Jesus' indwelling word (Holy Spirit in Jesus' followers).
9. Stott, *Between Two Worlds*, 101-102.

fresh application cannot be found from older familiar texts. What we are saying is that the contemporary voice of God should not be far removed from the written Word of God.

Each Testament of Scripture seems to affirm the above emphasis. What is preaching from the first (Old) testament? Preaching from the Old Testament might be defined as, "Explaining the Law in the context of God's redemptive story of delivering Israel, the covenant community, from bondage." The Levites and Bible teachers such as Ezra explained the ramifications of the Torah to the people (Neh 8:8), but that explanation was always in the context of God's salvific act. Moses, Joshua, and others put their theology in story (Deut 30:11-20; Josh 24:14-15). The contemporary voice of God for the people then was extrapolated from the written Word.

The Bible from its genesis is a speaking book.

The New Testament carries this contemporary voice of God that is honed to the written Word even further. We might define preaching from the New Testament as, "announcing the reign and government of Christ through his church for salvation and service." Preaching in the New Testament is more announcement than mere teaching.[10] Preaching is telling people what God has done in Christ and places the accent on the indicative. Indeed, there is a summons in New Testament preaching. There is implied imperative in New Testament preaching. But preaching, as far as the New Testament goes, clearly puts the accent on the indicative over the imperative.[11] God's contemporary voice is heard in announcing the Jesus story.

Knowing that through all the preacher's words will come God's Word helps us critique preaching through the Christian era so we can know when the text was winning and when it was not winning.[12] It also

---

10. It is very hard to draw a strong distinction between preaching and teaching. They might have a slightly different nuance when they appear together (e.g., Matt 4:23; 9:35), but they greatly overlap. C. H. Dodd might have overemphasized the distinction in his *Apostolic Preaching and Its Developments* (Grand Rapids: Baker, 1980).
11. We cannot get derailed with our historical sketch to deal with all the nuances of preaching. See chapter three for various terms such as preach, teach, witness, etc. Suffice it to say here that the hard-pressed distinctions between teaching and preaching advocated by C.H. Dodd and Alexander Campbell cannot be sustained. All good preaching contains content and substance, i.e., something for people to learn. And, all good teaching contains a hortatory element to challenge and inspire.
12. The early Christians *heard* the word, they *judged* the word, and they *were judged* by the word all at the same time (1 Cor 14:29-32; 1 Thess 2:13).

delivers us from puny discussions about "expository" versus "textual" versus "topical" kinds of labels.[13] Those labels might help preachers think through their sermon methodologies and be helpful for pedagogical purposes. But, at the end of the day, the deciding factor on what makes the text win is not the length of the chosen passage nor the method of treatment. It is whether or not the Word comes through the words. That is when the text wins.

The People and the Ideas

Given the constraints mentioned in footnote #2 of this chapter, we turn now to surveying a brief preaching history. Just like preachers can find their own preaching voice when they survey the many styles of preaching available, so preachers will want to find their place in this relay of truth.

In the Western Evangelical World several have offered contributions to the history of preaching. One of the most significant was Edwin C. Dargan's, *A History of Preaching*.[14] This was the standard work for some time. A similar work was Ralph Turnbull's, *A History of Preaching*.[15] Other works followed.[16] A quick survey of these sources reveals that the text did not always win. Sometimes rhetoric won. Sometimes western logic won. Sometimes allegory won. Sometimes tradition won. Sometimes dogma won. Sometimes human reason and higher criticism won. Sometimes psychology and therapy won. Sometimes culture won. And, sometimes the text won.

> God's... voice speaks through what he has already spoken. The Spirit takes the written Word and gives it a fresh hearing for today.

---

13. Stott, *Between Two Worlds*, says that all true Christian preaching is expository preaching (125-126). This is not descriptive of some kind of method but is referring to the sermon's content. "To expound is to bring out of the text what is there and expose it to view." (See this emphasis in chapter one.)
14. Edwin C. Dargan, *A History of Preaching*, 2 vol., repr. (Grand Rapids: Baker, 1968);
15. Ralph G. Turnbull, *A History of Preaching*, vol. 3 (Grand Rapids: Baker, 1974).
16. Frederick Roth Webber, *A History of Preaching in Britain and America* (Milwaukee: Northwestern, 1957); Warren W. Wiersbe and Lloyd M. Perry, *The Wycliffe Handbook of Preaching and Preachers* (Chicago: Moody, 1984); John MacArthur Jr., *Rediscovering Expository Preaching* (Dallas: Word, 1992); Clyde E. Fant and William M. Pinson, *20 Centuries of Great Preaching: An Encyclopedia of Preaching* (Waco, TX: Word, 1971); Paul Scott Wilson, *A Concise History of Preaching* (Nashville: Abingdon, 1992); William Willimon and Richard Lischer, *Concise Encyclopedia of Preaching* (Louisville, KY: Westminster John Knox, 1995); and Richard Lischer, ed., *The Company of Preachers: Wisdom on Preaching, Augustine to the Present* (Grand Rapids: Eerdmans, 2002).

Interfacing with the Greeks

As the Christian fellowship took seriously the marching orders of the Lord and spread throughout the Greco-Roman World, preaching interfaced with the rhetoric of the ancient Greeks. It did not escape unscathed. Christian sermons became more interested in how to say it than what was said. The church has always had a love/hate relationship with rhetoric (1 Cor 2:1-5). The influence of Plato's theory of knowledge and Aristotle's rhetoric cannot be overstated. Plato emphasized that objective realities here had higher counterparts in the world above. Aristotle put the accent on individual objects here and was concerned with arguments having a series of proofs. Thus the syllogism was identified. In an effort to "speak the language of the customer," sermons began to reflect this rhetoric and logical discourse. A few voices cried against this shift. Leaders like Justin Martyr, Tertullian, and Cyprian emphasized apologetics and argued against false doctrine that crept into the church via the influence of the Greeks.

Probing the Allegorizers

Christian preaching also struggled to maintain its integrity in the midst of an allegorical church. From the fourth century through the fifteenth century AD (often identified as the scholastic age and medieval period) the church was polarized in its hermeneutics and homiletics by the allegorization of the text. In one corner was the Alexandria (Egypt) School. This school of interpretation emphasized that the text has several layers of meaning that must be unpacked. There was the literal meaning, the moral meaning, the prophetic meaning, etc.[17] Most famous in this regard was Origen. While this period produced some famous preachers such as Peter the Hermit, Bernard of Clairvaux, and Thomas Aquinas, none of these preachers reversed this trend of not taking the text on its own terms.

The balance to the Alexandria School was the Antioch (Syria) School. Leaders in this school stood opposed to the extreme allegory of Alexandria. They wanted to understand the text, as much as possible, on its own terms, and therefore favored more simple expositions of Scripture. Preachers like John Chrysostom and Theodore of Mopsuestia

---

17. Let the record show that there is an allegorical emphasis in the Bible (Gal 4:21-31). Parables in particular have allegorical connections. See Craig Blomberg's book, *Interpreting the Parables* (Downers Grove, IL: InterVarsity, 1990). But this recognition is different from interpreting every passage allegorically, where hidden meanings, multiplicity of meanings, and odd connections are made to support some Greek theory of learning or ecclesiastical doctrine.

preached more from an authorial intent perspective and emphasized simple morality and common application. As the medieval period drew to a close, others such as John Wyclif, John Huss, and Girolamo Savonarola also became known for preaching the text on its own terms. They were assisted by scholars in the translation and hermeneutics fields such as Erasmus and John Colet.

While the scholastic age did give evidence of serious Bible study,[18] the church experienced many changes in leadership and in dogma. Preaching pastors became more entrapped in running the church in contrast to spending their time in the faithful exposition of Scripture. (Sound familiar?) The administration of the sacraments took center stage over the pulpit. The sermon was reduced to a shortened homily. Sermons became an exercise in poetry, and church dogma became more important than allowing the text to win. The word that comes to mind during this era was "control." The church controlled the people more than the text did.[19] Seth Wilson used to say, "All of our efforts to control people show our failure to convert them." When the text is winning, Holy Spirit conversion and transformation get the accent rather than ecclesiastical control.

> ...the deciding factor on what makes the text win... is whether or not the Word comes through the words. That is when the text wins.

Protesting with the Reformers

Several factors came together to set the stage for the text to once again get a fair hearing during the Reformation in Europe. In the church the linguistic work of Erasmus and others helped spark interest in the ancient text of Scripture. The work of Thomas Aquinas in emphasizing the place of human reason actually set the table for an informed faith.[20] In the culture there was a renewed interest in the arts and ancient Greek texts. There were also many serious social and political revolts.[21] In the midst of all of those changes the church had become corrupt. The

---

18. Not the least of which was the rise of concordance study.
19. The author is aware of how negative this sounds, especially to our Catholic and Greek Orthodox friends. There is no effort to be unkind or unfair. Obviously many good sermons were preached during this era, and the danger of a chapter like this is to unfairly stereotype people and events. In the main though we are suggesting that something other than the text was winning.
20. There were of course negative aspects to this idea of embracing reason over that of revelation. Francis Schaeffer always blamed Aquinas for taking the church off task as the Enlightenment began to dawn.
21. Such as the peasants revolt in Germany.

papacy hit rock bottom with its immorality and practice of indulgences. The stage was set for the text to win again.

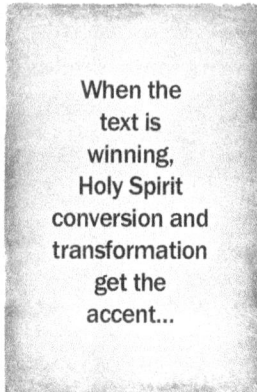

When the text is winning, Holy Spirit conversion and transformation get the accent...

Protest (thus Protestants) groups began springing up. Martin Luther, as well as other reformers such as John Calvin and Ulrich Zwingli, began to challenge the church from Scripture to define its doctrines.[22] Alongside of *Sola Dei Gloria*, *Sola Gratia*, and *Sola Fide* was *Sola Scriptura*. The text was allowed to speak unencumbered from church tradition. Luther wrote, "I simply taught, preached, wrote God's Word; otherwise I did nothing. . . . The Word did it all."[23] Zwingli said that he set about to preach simple didactic Bible lessons. He wanted to repeat the Word of God unabbreviated and unadulterated.[24] And even though Calvin wrote 45 volumes of commentaries, he prized clear brevity in his expositions.[25] We must beware of romanticizing the Reformation, and honesty forces us to admit that the post-Reformation era gave evidence of some of the same pitfalls in the Protestant Reformation that the Catholic Church had. However, the text had a very good day during the Reformation Movement.[26]

Watching the Homiletical Shifts

Tracing how the text won since the Reformation Movement is challenging at best. Forces such as American colonialism, the Enlightenment, the rise of biblical higher criticism, modernity, the preaching of the Puritans, the rising interest in the fields of psychology and philosophy, the spiritual awakenings in America, the rise of Pentecostalism, the therapeutic culture, and postmodernity all made

---

22. One advantage of the Reformation Movement in Europe for the Catholic Tradition was that it forced Rome to define its doctrines.
23. MacArthur, *Rediscovering*, 48.
24. Ibid.
25. Ibid., 49.
26. It would be appropriate at this point to commend historical surveys that championed preachers' fidelity to the Bible (as pointed out in works like John R. W. Stott's, *Between Two Worlds*, chapter one, 15-49, and John MacArthur's, *Rediscovering Expository Preaching*, chapter three, 36-60). While these chapters are thrilling to read, they make it sound as if any preacher in church history who said anything slightly in favor of the biblical text was a strong expositor and exemplary of how to preach so the text always won. But such is not the case universally. Haddon Robinson said that Charles Spurgeon preached all the right things from all the wrong texts. Is the text really winning in such cases? Since some sermon methodologies are preferable to others (see chapter seven) to ensure that the text is winning, sermon form does matter.

their challenges against letting the text win in the West.

But the promise of God was that, at the end of the day, the text really would win (Isa 55:10-11; 1 Pet 1:24-25). A preacher's belief in the sovereignty of God stands above both the content and form of the message. That is a good thing too. By the end of the nineteenth century and the beginning of the twentieth century a homiletical revolution that would shake the foundations of how the text would win began.[27]

John Broadus published his book, *On the Preparation and Delivery of Sermons*, in 1898.[28] This book was extremely popular, went through four major editions, and became the standard for generations of preachers. Broadus basically took an Aristotelian model of discourse and built a homiletical method on it. The text can and did win with this approach. Unfortunately it hammered most texts into a standard format. Sermons rang with sameness—not because of content but because of form.

In 1958 H. Grady Davis wrote a work that began a homiletical paradigm shift. It was entitled, *Design for Preaching*.[29] He argued that imposing an Aristotelian form on biblical texts was a violation of genre. The text already had a form, and preachers must respect that. He argued that the form of the text was part of the message.[30]

> ...the text had a very good day during the Reformation Movement.

Charles Koller's book, *Expository Preaching without Notes* (1962), pushed back on the new emphasis from Davis.[31] He made popular the "classification" approach to preaching. He would take a text and ask what plural key (noun) word best classifies the text (see chapter seven). The structure of the sermon would follow the lead of that plural key word. This little work was immensely

---

27. Space does not allow discussing the contributions of preachers like John Bunyan, John Wesley, George Whitefield, Charles H. Spurgeon, G. Campbell Morgan, Alexander Maclaren, Donald Barnhouse, Alexander Campbell, D. Martyn Lloyd-Jones, and John Stott.
28. John A. Broadus, *On the Preparation and Delivery of Sermons*, rev. by Vernon Stanfield (San Francisco: Harper and Row, 1979).
29. H. Grady Davis, *Design for Preaching* (Philadelphia: Fortress, 1958).
30. It should be noted that Davis' work predates Marshall McLuhan's famous work, *Understanding Media: The Extensions of Man* (New York: Signet Books, 1964) where we have the famous dictum, "The medium is the message."
31. This is not to imply that Koller was consciously trying to do that. It is interesting that Koller's book [*Expository Preaching without Notes* (Grand Rapids: Baker, 1962)] was published the same year that Thomas Kuhn's book, *The Structure of Scientific Revolutions*, repr.t (Chicago: University of Chicago Press, 1996) was published. Kuhn's book was pivotal and suggested that reality is viewed through a certain paradigm. To a great extent Koller's homiletical work worked with one paradigm.

popular for evangelical preachers, and it is still very ingrained in many sermons. It is a "bread and butter" way to craft a sermon. Preachers could do lots worse.

Then along came Fred Brenning Craddock. This New Testament scholar became a well-known preacher in the Disciples of Christ. Taking his cue from Davis' earlier work, he wrote his famous work, *As One without Authority*.[32] Craddock argued that much preaching is not very democratic. Preachers announce their theme at the beginning of the sermon. They have had all week to work on the text and theme. The congregation comes to the text and theme coldly and is simply asked to accept it. Craddock proposed that the sermon's movement should be in touch with the form of the text and that the sermon move inductively so the congregation can come to own the theme.[33] In other words, invert the typical Broadus approach. Put the supports first and then the conclusion, as opposed to the other way around.

> Craddock proposed... that the sermon move inductively so the congregation can come to own the theme.

This is the right spot to push the pause button on this brief historical sketch. Craddock emphasized that to the listener often a change in form sounds like a change in content. The text can win with inductive (indirect) or deductive (direct) approaches. But congregations reared on one method may hear a new method and conclude that the content was not *biblical*. To the ear of the church it sounded as if the text didn't win because the preacher chose a different approach to the text and theme. Reality might be that the text was winning in a greater way with the new approach than with the older one. But since the new approach sounded different the congregation concluded the text could not be winning.

Following the Tension between the Academy and the Society

The 1980s and 1990s brought a flurry of homiletical activity. As in most ages of the church the text would win during these decades with varying degrees of success. This activity can best be summarized by

---

32. Fred B. Craddock, *As One without Authority* (Nashville: Abingdon, 1971).
33. More could be said about inductive preaching. One of the clearest statements on it is David Enyart's chapter, "Inductive Proclamation: The Question, the Quest, and the Discovery," in *Preaching through Tears*, ed. by John D. Webb and Joseph G. Grana II (Lincoln, IL: 2000). Also see Ralph L. Lewis and Greg Lewis, *Inductive Preaching: Helping People Listen* (Westchester, IL: Crossway Books, 1983).

the two American homiletical societies. The Academy of Homiletics was actually begun in 1940, but it took some time for its effect to be felt.[34] Broadus and Koller were jettisoned. Craddock and Lowry[35] were embraced. Narrative and story were in. Proposition and linear outlines were out. The academy was composed primarily of homiletical scholars from mainline denominations. Without attempting to be cruel, their embrace of higher biblical criticism, reader response hermeneutics, and aspects of postmodernism were very evident. At times everything won but the text (e.g., someone's experience, an article from Reader's Digest, or some piece from a poet laureate). One of the more towering intellects in the academy was David Buttrick from Vanderbilt.[36] His work might represent where the academy has come philosophically.

The Evangelicals felt less at home with the direction of and the philosophical and hermeneutical constructs of the Academy. In the 1990s the Evangelical Homiletical Society began. The founders[37] desired to take advantage of the good literary insights discovered by the academy but stay more within the boundaries of biblical authority and authorial-intent hermeneutics. Three books show this in particular: The first is *Biblical Preaching* by Haddon Robinson[38] combined the hermeneutically discerned "big idea" (composed of the subject/complement)[39] with the insights gained from inductive and story methods of preaching. Dr. Robinson's sermon's construct looks like an hour glass. The introduction moves inductively until the delivering of the big idea. Then the rest of the sermon/text is taught deductively.[40]

---

34. The author attended his first Academy of Homiletics Meeting at Princeton Theological Seminary in 1990. It celebrated its 50th anniversary that year. Dr. Tom Long gave an address that traced the history of the homiletical work of the academy. To indicate the shift that had taken place, consider his two points: I. The Founders II. The Crazies. Everyone laughed when he announced his headings, but clearly a significant shift was being acknowledged in the teaching of homiletical method. Professors of homiletics who made up the academy were abandoning traditional methods of discourse in favor of new narrative and inductive methods. Time would tell whether or not the shift helped the text win in the sermon.
35. Eugene Lowry, *The Homiletical Plot* (Atlanta: John Knox, 1980).
36. His work, *Homiletic* (Philadelphia: Fortress, 1987), is still unsurpassed and is a profound statement about how language in a sermon works to create community through the moves and structures of public discourse.
37. People such as Keith Willhite, Scott Gibson, Jeffrey Arthurs, etc. Many of these homiletical teachers were students of Haddon Robinson.
38. Haddon Robinson, *Biblical Preaching: The Development and Delivery of Expository Messages* (Grand Rapids: Baker, 1980).
39. The subject answers the question, "What am I talking about?" The complement answers the question, "What am I saying about what I am talking about?"
40. Eugene Lowry would say that the cat gets out of the bag too early. Interest has peaked too soon. But strong biblical exposition and engaging illustrations and supports along the way can keep a congregation involved so the text can continue to win even after the big idea has been announced.

The second, Sidney Greidanus, professor at Calvin College and Seminary, was a member of the Academy of Homiletics. But his book, *The Modern Preacher and the Ancient* Text,[41] would not be typical of someone in the academy. He held out for reading the text on its own terms but added the art and genre sensitivity being discussed in the academy. He also set the stage for retaining the real Christocentric emphasis of the sermon, which gives rise to the third book.

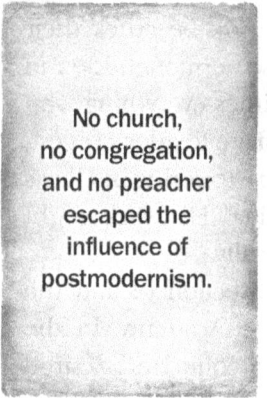

No church, no congregation, and no preacher escaped the influence of postmodernism.

The third is Bryan Chappell's book, *Christ-Centered Preaching*.[42] It was an effort to wed theological commitments to expositional work. This Seminary president stressed getting underneath the text to discern its FCF (fallen condition focus) so as to bring the redemptive element of the gospel to bear on the congregant.

There are, of course, a plethora of books on preaching. Each of them attempts to put some stress on letting the text win. Some seem more successful than others in this effort.[43] The two homiletical societies created two streams in terms of the text. Due to many of the philosophical presuppositions of the Academy of Homiletics, most members found a comfortable home in postmodernism. On the plus side of the ledger a strong emphasis was placed on the art and form of the text. Due to the theological commitments of the Evangelical Homiletical Society, most members stressed authorial-intent hermeneutics. On the plus side of the ledger a strong emphasis was placed on the authority and the *meantness* of the text.

New challenges for the text to win begin to emerge. Some of these challenges were a growing embrace of postmodernism as a worldview, a polarization of the political left and right, an existentialism and cultural relativism that turned up in every category of reality, a disagreement

---

41. Sidney Greidanus, *The Modern Preacher and the Ancient Text* (Grand Rapids: Eerdmans, 1986).
42. Bryan Chappell, *Christ Centered Preaching: Redeeming the Expository Sermon* (Grand Rapids: Baker, 1994).
43. We have not spoken about more modern sermonic approaches either here or in chapter seven such as Andy Stanley and Lane Jones, *Communicating for a Change* (Multnomah, OR: 2006). There is communicative value to a work like this and embracing his method. The "Me-We-God-You-We" imposed sermonic structure can be very engaging. Younger crowds seem especially hooked. Stanley's goal is not necessarily to teach a text but to transform a life. Worthy indeed. We raise two questions: 1) If the text is always to win, does that imposed structure actually violate the text at times? 2) Can the approach ring with sameness when we have such a wide variety of biblical genre from which to draw? These critiques are in no way to discredit Stanley as a very gifted communicator.

about how to read ancient and modern texts, and unbelievers showing up at church by the thousands.[44] How to let the text win in this pluralistic environment became the next hill to climb.[45]

The Times and the Shifts

Can the text win in the current postmodern climate? Can the text win in a culture where the locus of meaning has shifted from the text itself to the reader/hearer? Do preachers today preach *in* a postmodern world? Do they preach *with* a postmodern world? Or do they preach *as* postmoderns? The easiest question to answer is the first one because the answer is obvious. We have no choice.

No church, no congregation, and no preacher escaped the influence of postmodernism.[46] When the culture realized that modernity and its twin sisters, science and technology, could not save, it had the potential to work in the church's favor. But several other mitigating factors made the church's efforts in letting the text win gargantuan.

The first mitigating factor was the *place of truth*. To say that postmoderns are not interested in truth is way wide of the mark. Perhaps some "throw truth to the ground" (Dan 8:12), but many postmoderns are willing at least to talk about truth claims, even though those truth claims are all equal. For many what is typically referred to as objective truth is unknowable. Others claim that truth can be known,

> The Bible really does not get caught up in talking about truth as objective. It locates truth in a person.

---

44. Again it should be stressed that these phenomena were primarily in Western Christian Civilization. People in sub-Saharan Africa were not very worried about modernity and postmodernity. They wondered if they would have enough to eat tomorrow and whether or not they would get AIDS. Unbelievers showing up at church sounds like a good thing. But as the mega-church phenomenon continued to grow, seekers knew very little if any of the language of Zion. In the name of helping people maintain their anonymity and not offending people, the church in many sectors all but lost the theological "insider" talk. This might be referred to as the tension between Willow and Willimon. The megachurch in South Barrington, Illinois, wants to make fully devoted disciples of Jesus. Much of their method in the early days of the church was to avoid offense at any level so as not to lose a good opportunity to influence that person for the gospel. They desired to "speak the language of the customer." Others, such as William Willimon, former dean of the chapel at Duke University, didn't seem to care whom the gospel offended. In fact, for Willimon, the offense was the very thing that made the gospel attractive.
45. This is stated well by a former co-worker and personal friend, Jim Johnson. He said that for Lowry (as in Eugene Lowry) the gospel is the answer. For Willimon (as in William Willimon) the gospel is the problem.
46. It is hard to improve on Jean-Francis Lyotard's definition of postmodernism. It is only three words long, but it is quite complete. He defines it as "incredulity toward metanarrative." Jean-Francis Lyotard, "The Postmodern Culture: A Report on Knowledge," *Theory of Knowledge* (Minneapolis: University of Minnesota, 1984).

but it is only subjectively discerned and probably oppressive.

The second mitigating factor was the *place of experience*. Rationalism was jettisoned, and experience was enthroned. Since experiences are so varied, ambiguity is prized and postmoderns seem happy to live with seeming contradictions. Experience is full of emotion and not dependent on cold logic.

The third mitigating factor was the *place of spirituality*. Do not think this spirituality is necessarily Christian. Spirituality is varied and multiple. It is ever evolving. Therefore there is a distrust of organized religion, and the obligation of everyone is to be tolerant of other people's spirituality.

The fourth mitigating factor was the *place of language*. Basically language is an inadequate conduit to deliver information. Language is socially conditioned and therefore can be oppressive. So for communication and meaning to take place the language has to be deconstructed.[47]

The fifth mitigating factor was the *place of morality*. Morality in a postmodern situation is existential. It is negotiable and not fixed. It can become sensual and animalistic.[48]

These mitigating factors might seem insurmountable for the text to win. Actually it is just the opposite. The biblical text speaks in all and to all of the mitigating factors. The Bible really does not get caught up in talking about truth as objective. It locates truth in a person. The biblical text does not fear experience. Rather it embraces experience. The biblical text admits that there are many spiritualities in a fallen world (1 Corinthians 8). But it locates that spirituality in Christian community. The biblical text would admit that language is a not a perfect medium for communication (1 Corinthians 13). But even with potential for great misunderstanding

---

47. Two personal instances underline the inadequacy of this position. 1) George Will told of the philosophy professor who lectured all hour on how all meaning is indeterminate. After class he went down the hallway to his office, called his wife and requested pepperoni pizza for dinner, and never saw the contradiction. 2) A composer from NPR told a concert audience of what he was trying to communicate in the four moves of his piece of music. The music was attempting to tell the story of the composer's brother who had been diagnosed with cancer. The four moves highlighted the emotions of the brother (shock, despair, anger, and acceptance). The four students in the string quartet from Julliard played the piece of music beautifully. But the composer said several times, "Now when I compose a piece of music I release it. You can interpret it any way you wish. However what I was trying to say was..." The old adage of, "Me thinks thou protesteth too much" comes to mind. In other words, we might attempt, in light of our proclaimed philosophy, to say that meaning is located only in the hearer, but reality is that we communicate with others every day. And, we expect people to understand us in the way we meant to be understood. Evidently not all meaning is indeterminate.
48. Ravi Zacharias made five similar points in a sermon entitled, "An Ancient Message through Modern Means to a Postmodern Mind." [Jonathan Kever, ed. *Great Preaching* (Jackson, TN: The Preaching Library, 2002)]. He said in a truly postmodern climate: 1) Philosophy moves to the existential. 2) Art moves to the sensual. 3) Religion moves to the mystical. 4) Education moves to the skeptical. 5) Individual moves to the transcendental.

people go about their days, for the most part, understanding each other quite well.

Actually the text can win in postmodern settings, postmodern culture, and postmodern times. Postmodernism as a worldview tends to cave in on itself. It uses reason (and many other things) to deny reason. At the end of the day the gospel (and the biblical text) has the kind of explaining power to still make the things of earth grow strangely dim. It is beyond the scope of this chapter to offer a critique of postmodernism.[49] Our confidence remains in the biblical text. The text survived the persecution, the early heresies, the dark ages, the crusades, the split between eastern and western Christianity, the Reformation, the Enlightenment, existentialism, modernity, and it will survive (maybe even thrive under) postmodernity. It is varied enough to speak to all the particulars of a diverse world. It contains the only glue to mend east and west.

> ...let us eliminate any unnecessary offensive method of communcation that would place an obstacle in people's path on route to the cross.

Conclusion

Preachers who want to let the text win will preach the text and let the chips fall off the postmodern log where they will. We announce the Jesus story. It is the power and wisdom of God (1 Corinthians 1). One way to ensure that the text will get its appropriate hearing and therefore win is to eliminate any needless offensive ways in our presentations of the text. Let the offense remain in the gospel/text. But let us eliminate any unnecessary offensive method of communication that would place an obstacle in people's path on route to the cross. (See Appendix A for some practical help in this regard).

---

49. Many books do this. David Lose, *Confessing Jesus Christ: Preaching in a Postmodern World* (Grand Rapids: Eerdmans, 2003); Kevin J. Vanhoozer, ed., *The Cambridge Companion to Postmodern Theology* (Cambridge: Cambridge University Press, 2003); Stanley J.A. Grenz, *A Primer on Postmodernism* (Grand Rapids: Eerdmans, 1996); Graham Johnston, *Preaching to a Postmodern World: A Guide to Reaching Twenty-First Century Listeners* (Grand Rapids: Baker, 2001); David C. Henderson, *Culture Shift: Connecting God's Truth to Our Changing World* (Grand Rapids: Baker, 1998). A recent gold mine of practical preaching advice on this subject is found in Darrell W. Johnson's, *The Glory of Preaching: Participating in God's Transformation of the World* (Downers Grove, IL: InterVarsity, 2009), especially 224-233. Johnson reminds us that postmodernism is really quite local (in the West). It is not nearly as significant in the East or South. Also, in efforts to adjust our message to the postmodern scene we might subtly undermine the gospel. In our overeffort to be relevant we may lose the very message we want to share. Johnson reminds us to "read the Times, but more so read the Eternities" (201).

my thoughts than my thoughts.

10 "For as the rain and the snow come down from heaven, and return not thither but water the earth, making it bring forth and sprout, giving seed to the sower and bread to the eater, shall my word be that goes forth from my mouth; it shall not return to me empty, it shall accomplish that which I purpose, and prosper in the thing for which I sent it.

u shall go out in joy, e led forth in peace; ntains and the hills before reak forth into singing, he trees of the field shall eir hands. he thorn sh

CHAPTER 3
LETTING THE TEXT WIN OVER THE PREACHER (JK)

Perhaps this is a strange question for a preaching textbook, but it must be asked in light of the urgency of the day: How does the preacher become convinced of preaching? I have often asked my students why they are at a Christian college preparing to preach. Some will say, "I sense a calling from God." Others will offer, "My youth minister persuaded me to come. He thought I had gifts for the preaching and teaching ministry." A few will openly admit, "I didn't have anything else to do and didn't know where else to go." Now and then I will come across this really transparent and honest student who will say something like this, "I don't know what I'm doing here. I had a scholarship to the university. I can't explain how I got here, but I just see the mess of the world and I wonder if I could be used of God in whatever He is doing. I believe He is at work, and I'd like to partner with Him." Usually when I hear that kind of response I want to stop class and hug that person and pray that I won't ruin what God has clearly started.

Somewhere in my years of teaching I came to the conclusion that I could not force students to become preachers. I admit my wholehearted passion about speaking on behalf of God, but I'm not very good at recruiting the undecided to want to preach. I probably have done more of the opposite. I have convinced some young men and women they ought to consider doing something else! I have even gone so far as to ask students to drop out as preaching majors due to a lack of appropriate giftedness or the presence of inappropriate character. I do confess that preaching and teaching is in my blood. It keeps me awake at night and whispers to me in the morning. I love talking about it, reading about it, hearing it, and doing it. I am a preacher. I am honored, humbled, and called to carry on the most important task in the history of the world.

I encourage and insist that all would-be preachers take the necessary time to read, meditate on and pray over four gigantic New Testament passages. These texts are Romans 10:1-15, 1 Corinthians 1:18–2:5, Ephesians 4:8-16, and 2 Timothy 3:10–4:5. I plead with them to get these passages into their preacher's bones. The soul, heart, and mind of the preacher need to be saturated with these great Bible sections. The entire chapter of Romans 10 reminds us why religion can't save us. The apostle tells the church in Rome that religion can be sincere, but sincerity is not enough. Religion is full of self, but self is not enough. Religion is safe, but being safe is not enough. At the heart of Romans 10 Paul does something profoundly paradoxical. He elevates six key verbs and then places them in reverse order: save, call, believe, hear, preach, and send (10:13-15).The truth of the matter is that preachers are sent and preach, people hear and believe, then call on the Lord and are saved. Paul's point is that all of this is about God and His great power and not our own. God makes the gospel accessible and reasonable. The preacher is a privileged mouthpiece who gets to partner alongside God the evangelist!

> I am honored, humbled, and called to carry on the most important task in the history of the world.

Paul works from a different angle when he speaks to the Christian Church in Corinth, Greece. He knows all about their divisions, arguments, and questions. At the very beginning he reminds them of God's faithfulness (1:9). Paul tells them boldly and yet graciously that God set aside the world's wisdom by the cross (1:18-25), by choosing the Corinthians (1:26-31), and by the weakness of preaching (2:1-5). Meditate on this great text. Ask yourself, "What would a model preacher look like?" Notice Paul's response. He would say that it is not about the preacher being flawless, flamboyant, or entertaining. The model preacher is consumed with God's power. Paul resolved to shape his preaching with plain words, simplicity, humility, and a complete reliance on God's power. The Corinthian church was in a mess and Paul's perspective was that God's power displayed through biblical preaching would hold that congregation together. First Corinthians 1:18–2:5 is a magnificent reminder that Jesus alone is the primary subject of all of our preaching and teaching.

If Paul's relationship with the Corinthians was at times shaky, then his relationship with the Christian community in Ephesus was rock solid. This church-planting-preacher reminded the Ephesians that they were a part of God's colossal global plan for reconciling the world to Himself. He uses breathless language to attempt to describe the nearly indescribable (1:1-14). He is honest and gracious when he says that all of us are dead when Jesus doesn't live in us (2:1-3). He is just as honest and gracious when he says that all of us become alive when Jesus offers us His grace and we accept (2:4-10).

Paul clearly and concisely tells us how the church is to respond to pagan culture. He discloses what was once hidden. Jews and Gentiles are now heirs together in all the promises wrapped up in Jesus. Because of this we are to maintain the unity that God has already given us in Christ (3:1-16). The church is already united. Now the gigantic task is to live like it. It is by our living out this unity and being God's PowerPoint to a watching world that we penetrate the pagan culture for Jesus Christ. It is God's unlimited power once again that makes all this possible (3:20-21). Ephesians 4:8-16 tells us that God gave leadership gifts to the church. The objective was to make it possible for leaders to partner with God in putting broken lives back together, so that ministry could be shared. The goal of all of this is Christian maturity.

It would be immensely beneficial to take the time right now to look at the two images Paul uses in 4:14. He speaks of the ocean and the wind. His hope is that mature disciples could be formed who have their sea legs, who can lean into the wind of pagan culture and false teaching. He wants to make the kind of disciple who isn't knocked off his feet by rough water or strong wind. It is at this point that the preacher must really tune in. Paul tells the reader that the appropriate response is to speak the truth in love (4:15). Maturity and unity are realities when someone regularly and consistently speaks loving truth.

It is tragic that the fourth great text, 2 Timothy 3:10–4:5, is often read only at ordination services. Some even make it an elitist passage intended only for those who are paid to preach. Paul describes for Timothy what a purpose-driven servant leader really looks like. A purpose-driven servant leader looks like someone who passionately remains faithful in a lifelong commitment to Scripture. I sometimes ask my students, "Do you ever get tired of hearing Paul say that over and over?" Paul declares, "But as for you, *continue* in what you have learned and become convinced of" (3:14). Timothy is to be different from the impostors of his day. The vocabulary suggests that the preacher is to stay, remain, and abide in the Scriptures. Anyone who wants to be a purpose-driven servant leader must be careful of chasing fads, of pursuing the latest gimmick to make the church more relevant to the culture. Paul takes the time to tell Timothy about the Scripture's origin and purpose (3:16-17). It would be wise to let these verses incubate in your mind. Please notice that Paul charges Timothy and us to share the Scripture (4:2). It is urgent and relevant—just say what God has said. The word for "charge" (4:1) (*diamartyromai*) is a courtroom word. It means that Paul is placing Timothy under oath: "Do you solemnly swear that you will tell the truth, the whole truth, and nothing but the truth, so help you God?" What a magnificent question for any preacher!

> It is by our living out this unity and being God's PowerPoint to a watching world that we penetrate the pagan culture for Jesus Christ.

These four passages give us a foundation for all of our preaching, but we still have not really answered a fundamental question. What is Christian preaching? Most Bible colleges and seminaries have a course that offers basic principles for learning how to preach the gospel. In some schools this course is called "Homiletics." Homiletics is actually a word drawn from the Greek language. It literally means "to say the same thing." For those of us who preach it means to say the same thing as the biblical text. Preaching, therefore, becomes the art and discipline of preparing and delivering sermons that say what the biblical text says. The New Testament is not short on vocabulary that reminds us how wide and large this preaching business really is. The following verbs can have an enormous impact over the life of the one who is serious about letting the text win.

Major Terms

1. **Preach (*Kerusso*):** This essential term originally painted the picture of a town messenger (noun – *kerux*) who shouted out the news of the day in a strategic spot. The word also disclosed the picture of a herald bringing the king's message to the people. He was entrusted with the task of saying exactly what he had been told to say. *Kerusso* is the term used to describe what Jesus did (Mark 1:45). It is what Noah did in his day (2 Pet 2:5). It is what angels do in the book of Revelation (12:10-12; 14:6-7; 19:5-8). It is what we are called to do (2 Tim 4:2). I so deeply appreciate the reminder of Alger Fitch:

   > A herald is not one sent to give a personal discourse on some religious theme. He is not a person who is free

to express his personal views concerning any number of themes on which he holds strong opinions. He has not been commissioned to recite anecdotes, personal experiences or the latest jokes he has heard at the office. A herald is not even intended to lead discussions by the public about topics of general interest. . . . Let the modern proclaimer of the King of kings make known far and wide the news from King Jesus (*What the Bible Says about Preaching*, 14-15).

2. **Teach (*Didasko*):** This beautiful word is best understood as explaining Scripture in light of Jesus. It literally means to give instruction. Any good preacher or teacher combines these first two terms into a seamless witness. When we preach we teach, and when we teach we preach. This term is also used of Jesus. The Bible declares, "Jesus went throughout Galilee, teaching . . ." (Matt 4:23). It is the very thing that the first-century preachers, Paul and Barnabas, did (Acts 15:35). Again, if we are to be made in the likeness of the New Testament preachers, then this is our calling too (Matt 28:18-20 and Mark 16:16).

3. **Evangelize (*Euangelizo*):** I love this word. It means to bear good news or offer news that is filled with joy! Those of us who preach are greatly blessed to share the news of God's mighty activity in and through Jesus Christ! Hallelujah! What is being emphasized in the New Testament usage of this word is the content of the message. Jesus claimed that He was anointed to do this very thing (Luke 4:18). The noun "evangelist" may help us to see what the New Testament writers intended for those of us who speak on behalf of God. Paul reminded Timothy that he was to do the work of an evangelist. The context in which he shares this is a preaching and teaching context (2 Tim 4:5). At the very heart of proclamation is the loud vibration of good news. God did something for us that we could not do for ourselves.

> Preaching... therefore becomes the art and discipline of preparing and delivering sermons that say what the biblical text says.

4. **Exhort/Edify (*Parakaleo*):** The New Testament calls all Jesus-followers to encourage one another (1 Thess 4:18; 5:11; Heb 3:13; 10:25).

I am greatly blessed when I consider that the noun form of this word (*paraklete*) is one of the primary words for the Holy Spirit (John 14:16). He is the great encourager! We are privileged to partner with Him in walking alongside people and cheering them on. Our task is to urge and exhort. When we preach, we have the chance to put our arms around people with our words and build them up in their relationship with Jesus.

5. **Admonish (*Noutheteo*):** This is not a difficult word to understand. It simply means to warn or to encourage. When we share positive truth from Scripture, we place that idea into the mind of those who listen. In Acts 20:31 the Apostle Paul challenged the Ephesian elders, "Remember that for three years I never stopped *warning* each of you night and day with tears" (Acts 20:31). Every time we preach there is an element of this word in our message.

6. **Say (*Lego*):** I include this word in our discussion because it carries some heavy weight. At first appearance this little verb doesn't seem to have much punch. The truth of the matter, however, is that big things do come in small packages. The word is often used to denote the giving of a special speech. A great example of this is found in Matthew 11:25. Jesus is teaching and preaching in the towns of Galilee. The Gospel writer says, "At that time Jesus *said* . . . ." Matthew then records the speech. Over and over again, this tiny word is attached to the significant preaching ministry of Jesus. The Sermon (teaching) on the Mount contrasts Jesus six times with the religious teachers of the day: "You have heard that it was said . . . ." "But I *tell* you . . . ." (Matt 5:21-22,27-28,31-32,33-34,38-39,43-44). Jesus is saying, "You have heard how this is interpreted, but here is how I interpret this . . . ." What Jesus says reveals His deity! These are monumental christological declarations! Every time we preach, we echo something of what Jesus has already said.

7. **Prophesy (*Propheteuo*):** There probably have been more fights and arguments over this preaching term than any other. What a tragedy that such a clarifying word could promote such profound confusion. The preacher who honestly and reverently studies this word typically comes to the conclusion that the idea behind the word is more about forth-telling the truth than about foretelling the future. I know when a huddle of Christian people begin talking about what they mean by

"prophetic preaching," there are multiple viewpoints. The verb simply means to say something in the name of God. A prophet is someone who speaks on behalf of God. When I study 1 Corinthians 14, I come to the conclusion that the gift of prophecy is an intelligent, oral, clear, and Spirit-directed speaking of God's Word. The sixteenth-century reformers, Calvin and Luther, thought of prophecy as having to do with sermon-making and preaching.

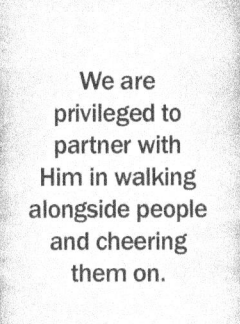

We are privileged to partner with Him in walking alongside people and cheering them on.

8. **Witness (*Martureo*):** Preaching as witness means to attest, testify, confirm, or speak well of something or someone. Our contemporary perspective leads us immediately to think of someone dying for their faith, someone martyred in the name of Jesus. This muscular word, though, is about witnessing or testifying to the reality of Christ in our life. It fascinates me to hear Jesus witness of Himself to Nicodemus (John 3:11). The apostles in Acts are constantly witnessing in their preaching and teaching (Acts 1:3,21-22; 10:40-41; 22:14-15; and 26:16). Of course, all of us are limited by our understanding of Jesus. The story is bigger than any one of us. Yet we tell the truth of our experience through our own personality every time we preach.

9. **Refute/Reason (*Dialegomai*):** This is one of Dr. Luke's favorite terms as he records for us the story of the early church, specifically Paul's preaching (Acts 17:2,17; 18:4,19; 19:8,9; 20:7,9; 24:12,25). Paul made it one of his ministry priorities to enter into the local synagogue and reason with those who were there. The idea behind the word is that a hearty discussion occurs and/or a debate arises. Good sermons create healthy discussions.

10. **Word (*Logos*):** I don't know if there is a more important preaching term than this one. It is a word that describes God's great creative and redemptive power as seen in Jesus. So often we think of this word only in light of John 1:1 and 14, "In the beginning was the Word and the Word was with God and the Word was God. . . . The Word became flesh . . . ." That section of Scripture offers enough power and punch for me to want to preach the rest of my days. However, I especially delight in how Peter uses this term to make me think of its

legitimate place in preaching and teaching. Peter says, "But in your hearts set apart Christ as Lord. Always be prepared to give an answer to everyone who asks you to give the *reason* (a word) for the hope that you have. But do this with gentleness and respect . . ." (1 Pet 3:15). That picture challenges me and blesses me at that same time. My hope and prayer is that it would be a blessing to you.

Minor Terms

There are some minor terms that should be noted. This does not mean they are not important, but are simply not as vital or significant to our discussion. These words include: Tell, speak boldly, strengthen, reprove/rebuke, reveal/disclose, shout, persuade, describe, explain/open, prove, address, feed, acknowledge/confess, spread, etc.

So, what does all this mean in light of allowing the text to win over the heart and mind of the preacher? If the text is to win over the preacher, at least four applications are needed.

First, the preacher must never forget the source of his preaching. Preaching at its very core is divine truth. This is a major premise for me. The Bible is the Word of God to people. It is God's grand narrative for putting the broken and fractured world, all of it, back together. It is one thing to believe God has acted, but it is another to believe that He has first spoken. Because He has spoken we can speak. All Christians, who are true Jesus-followers, believe that God did something wonderfully, mysteriously, and uniquely in Jesus. God first spoke this divine truth through His prophets and ultimately spoke it through Jesus Christ Himself (Heb 1:1-3). This is where preaching begins to energetically surface. God has revealed Himself. He has spoken. The message we bring originates with Him. Any authority we bring is found in Him alone! We are privileged mouthpieces. Listeners are responsible because our source is the Creator of the universe!

> "Great preachers are good communicators, but good communicators are not necessarily great preachers."

To reject the message of the preacher, if it is accurately shared, is not to reject the preacher, but the One who sent him. Therefore, I can preach with confidence because my authority, my source is found in God Himself!

Second, the preacher must never forget the substance of what is preached. All New Testament preaching is grace-centered. At the heart of all the vocabulary that we have considered is this gigantic and awesome storm of grace. God has acted first. He did something first. He gave something first. He spoke first. Preaching, more than anything, should express God's great lover's heart, His immense concern for people. My bias is a strong one. I believe that preaching should always instill a deeper sense of the grace of God. I agree with all those who have humbly acknowledged, "Preaching is not just getting something off my chest, it is getting something of God's grace into the heart."

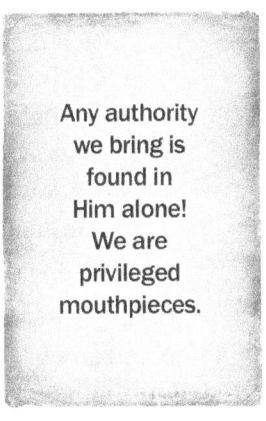

Any authority we bring is found in Him alone! We are privileged mouthpieces.

Third, the preacher cannot forget that what he does is absolutely necessary. The divine truth leads us to divine grace, which leads us to a divine compulsion. The church needs biblical preaching like the human race needs oxygen, water, and food. There is a law of threes that reminds me of this urgency. Most of us cannot survive more than three minutes without oxygen, more than three days without water, or more than three weeks without food. The church cannot survive three seconds without the faithful exposition of God's Word. Walter Kaiser has helped me enormously. "The cure for many of the ills afflicting the church and the seminaries of the day is to be found in the faithful exposition of the Word of God. Faithfulness in this area is the primary prerequisite for alleviating the deepest concerns currently held by the church and society" (*Preaching and Teaching from the Old Testament*). Karl Barth reminded the church in the last century that she must continually be occupied with the exposition and application of Scripture (See *Dogmatics in Outline*). Preaching is necessary because the church must be fed nutritious meals regularly. Preaching is necessary because the church needs clarity and direction in a time of great cultural darkness. Preaching is necessary because it leads the listener to salvation and maturity. Preaching is necessary because it changes the heart of the preacher. We are compelled by God, by the Scriptures, by the conviction of the Holy Spirit, by Christ's model, and by the mess of the world to reveal God's revelation of Himself in Jesus. Clyde Fant needs to be heard,

> Preaching is not essential to the church or to theology because the church has always done it, or because

the early apostles did it, or even because Jesus did it. Preaching continues to have an irreplaceable position in Christian theology and Christian worship because it does what God did in His self-disclosure to Israel, in His revelation to prophets and apostles, in the fullness of His revelation in Jesus. It provides a medium for revelation which enables the eternal Word to maintain its living, dynamic character and encounter our concrete situation. (*Preaching for Today*, 26)

Amen and amen.

Fourth, the one who would preach cannot forget that this great task is historical. Anyone who takes up the preaching baton and runs the good race is entering into a holy legacy. Please let that sink in. Dwell on that statement. Every time we preach we enter into that great relay of truth that includes John Chrysostom, Bernard of Clairvaux, John Wyclif, Martin Luther, John Knox, George Whitefield, John Wesley, Robert McCheyne, John Jasper, Alexander Campbell, Barton Stone, D.L. Moody, Martin Luther King, Jr., James S. Stewart, Harry Emerson Fosdick, Billy Graham, Gardner Taylor, James Earl Massey, E.V. Hill, Fred Craddock, Haddon Robinson, John Ortberg, Tony Evans, Mark Driscoll, Bill Hybels, Francis Chan, Andy Stanley, Dave Stone, Mike Baker, Matt Chandler, Ed Young, Aaron Brockett, Kyle Idleman, Jon Weece, Deveraux Hubbard, and so many others, including my coauthor and friend, Mark Scott, and you. We have a majestic history! Sometimes this heritage, this rich preaching genealogy will be the only thing that will see you through the dry seasons. You will persevere, because they persevered! Each time I stop and ponder the enormous size of all of this, I am reminded of the eternal nature of preaching. What we do has eternal implications. Because of this I can't think of anything that is more relevant! Preaching touches the living situation like nothing else can.

> Craddock proposed... that the sermon move inductively so the congregation can come to own the theme.

I confess to you that I did not want to preach. I absolutely hated it when the elderly ladies in the church would come up to me and tell me that one day I would preach like my father. I ran from the idea. I did everything I could to disqualify myself. But I am here to tell you that the Word of

God won me over. God called me, visited me, and put me back together. I love meditating on the words of E.M. Bounds. "The preacher on whom God's power descends must be marked by loyalty to God's Word. The Holy Ghost cannot and will not sanction by His approval disloyalty to God's Word. The preacher must accept and act on the statement that 'God has magnified His Word above all His name.' And he must hold God's Word in this high and unchallenged eminence and never veer from it" (Darrel King, *Men of Faith: E.M. Bounds*, 18). My abiding prayer is that the Word of God will win you over.

> Anyone who takes up the preaching baton and runs the good race is entering into a holy legacy... great relay of truth...

my thoughts higher than thoughts than

10 "For as the rain and the snow come down from heaven, and return not thither but water the earth, making it bring forth and sprout, giving seed to the sower and bread to the eater, shall my word be that goes forth from my mouth; it shall not return to me empty, it shall accomplish that which I purpose, and prosper in the thing for which I sent it.

you shall go out in joy, and be led forth in peace; the mountains and the hills before you shall break forth into singing, and the trees of the field shall clap their hands.

CHAPTER 4
LETTING THE TEXT WIN IN THE STUDY: Part 1 (JK)

Study matters. Mark and I believe it matters so much that we have devoted two chapters to discussing it. Let's begin this part of the conversation with the wise words of Charles Spurgeon, "Sermons should have real teaching in them" (*Lectures to His Students*, 61). Of course, most of us would ask, "How can that be possible unless we spend quality time studying the biblical text?" Yet there is a real and hidden danger in that question. Nearly thirty years ago, Dr. Fred Craddock got me thinking about that camouflaged land mine.

> When the life of study is confined to 'getting up sermons,' very likely those sermons are undernourished. They are the sermons of a preacher with the mind of a consumer, not a producer, the mind that looks upon life in and out of books in terms of usefulness for next Sunday. . . . Studying only for the next sermon is very much like clearing out of the wilderness a small garden patch, only to discover the next week that the wilderness has again taken over. (*Preaching*, 69)

What I want to talk about in this chapter is the development of a lifetime of study that deepens the preacher, as well as the congregation. This is the place where who we really are and what we really believe is shaped.

The New Testament has a word it likes to use when it wants to describe someone intimately attached to Jesus. The most common term for that kind of attachment is "disciple." The Gospel writers and Luke's second volume, Acts, record some 264 usages of the word. Study and discipleship go hand in hand. When these two words are cemented together, study becomes an act of obedience to God, an act of love toward the community of believers we serve, an act of listening to collective wisdom, and of course, an act of worship. Richard Foster would remind us that many Jesus-followers:

remain in bondage to fears and anxieties simply because they do not avail themselves of the discipline of study. They may be faithful in church attendance and earnest in fulfilling their religious duties and still they are not changed. I am not here speaking only of those who are going through mere religious forms, but of those who are genuinely seeking to worship and obey Jesus Christ as Lord and Master. They may sing with gusto, pray in the Spirit, live as obediently as they know how ... and yet the tenor of their lives remains unchanged. Why? Because they have never taken up one of the central ways God uses to change us: study. (*Celebration of Discipline*, 54)

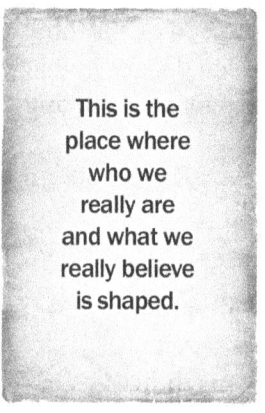

This is the place where who we really are and what we really believe is shaped.

Donald Whitney echoes that high view of study (*Spiritual Disciplines for the Christian Life*, 213-219). There must be a commitment to a whole life of study in which we are not accidental or sporadic learners, but intentional and systematic, ongoing learners. Apprentices to Jesus study at His feet.

There are multiple reasons why a lifelong commitment to study is so important for the preacher. First, it is one of the main tools God the Spirit uses to shape our character and deepen our faith. The Holy Spirit's power and presence is essential to the entire task of proclamation. He is at work in our study as He helps in our preparation. He is at work in the pulpit through our words, thoughts, creativity, imagination, pace, and passion. Our deliberation is dependent upon Him.

He is also at work in the pew through illumination. He awakens the bored, confronts the compromising, feeds the hungry, and encourages the wounded. I love contemplating the truth of Spurgeon's old words.

> I believe in the Holy Ghost. . . . Our hope of success, and our strength for continuing the service, lie in the belief that the Spirit of the Lord rests upon us. . . . To us, as ministers, the Holy Spirit is absolutely essential. . . . It is in our study-work, in that blessed labor when we are alone with the Book before us, that we need the help of the Holy Spirit. . . . If you study the original, consult the commentaries, and meditate deeply, yet if you neglect

to cry mightily unto the Spirit of God your study will not profit you. (*Lectures to His Students*, 171-175)

All of our study and all of our preaching requires absolute dependence on God the Spirit!

Second, a lifelong commitment to study keeps us from being seduced by our own opinions and prejudices. All of us are prone toward exegetical and hermeneutical bias. Good study offers us a second and third opinion. It affords us the opportunity to have our thoughts and viewpoints challenged. I used to joke that my father could find the theme of baptism in any biblical passage. He cared so deeply about communicating the New Testament norm for becoming a disciple of Jesus Christ that it seemed as if he stressed it in every sermon. I confess that my own years of preaching have birthed some of my own pet themes and favorite topics. I tend to want to read those subjects into every biblical text that I preach, but good study stands like a bouncer at the door, checking to make sure I have not added or taken away anything that was not already there.

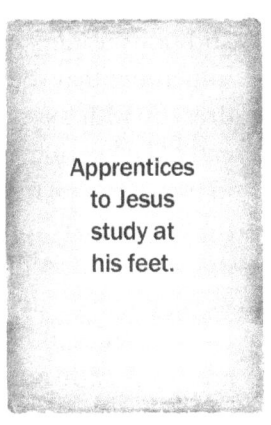

Apprentices to Jesus study at his feet.

Third, a commitment to lifelong study cultivates deep conviction and firm confidence. Fred Lybrand puts it this way in his good and helpful book, *Preaching On Your Feet*. "The fire and heartbeat in a sermon are formed in the preparation, not in the moment. If a preacher is to preach with earnestness and intensity, with fire and heart, then he must acquire the burden of the message in the preparation" (98). The preacher that prayerfully and studiously pores over the biblical text finds that he not only has something to say from God, but he discovers that his mind and heart are set on fire. People will want to hear what he has to say. If for no other reason, they will come and watch him burn up to the glory of God! Several years ago my wife and I were in Dallas, Texas, and had the blessed opportunity to hear Chuck Swindoll preach at the Evangelical Free Church in Frisco. He was wrestling with a difficult passage, and I was struck by the fact that his thorough study had made it possible for him to approach the passage with humility, but also with boldness. He knew the text was bigger than he was, but he also found a quiet confidence that allowed him to declare what he believed that passage was saying.

Fourth, the kind of study we are talking about keeps our listeners fresh and full. Our study will be larger than our sermon. We will avoid that terrible trap of only studying enough to find a sermon for next Sunday. I tell my students that good study is a lot like grilling hamburgers and brats. I want a piece of meat that goes far beyond the bun. I want something that you do not have to search for with a magnifying glass or dress up with lots of condiments in order to have something satisfying to eat! I like hearing a sermon in which I know the preacher could say a lot more about that text than is revealed in the sermon. I want the preacher's study to be so completely full and fresh that I walk away wanting to study that passage myself. I want the listener to walk out of that auditorium and worship experience with the overwhelming sense that God has spoken.

Of course, these reasons for remaining committed to lifelong study are filled with potential potholes and distractions. There are clearly several challenges to the life of study. The wonders of technology—the smart phone, computer, iPAD, palm-pilot, and all sorts of other gadgets—can actually get in the way of our study. They can occupy our time more than the biblical text. Our own personalities can slow us down. Some of us want to spend all of our time with people, and some of us give our attention to the loudest demand. The congregation's own expectations can hamper us. I have been drawn away from study on numerous occasions because someone wanted to ask me a question or meet with me to discuss something or have me pray with them because of some difficulty they were facing.

Sometimes our own bad experiences in developing and cultivating good study habits can slow us down in this lifelong pursuit. My fifth grade teacher, who shall remain nameless, nearly killed any desire I had for study. She made everything twice as hard by threatening, bullying, and embarrassing her students. Why she ever chose the teaching field I will never know. I have a vivid picture of her stomping into the classroom like she had just walked off the Mayflower and was not happy about the boat ride or the company she had kept. She seemed irritated at the whole world! Only because I had a few exceptional teachers did my desire to read and study have a fighting chance.

> ...good study stands like a bouncer at the door, checking to make sure I have not added or taken away anything that was not already there.

Some of us find the life of study challenging for altogether different reasons. We have grown up in a church that values spontaneity and does not support anything that smells of real preparation. Some have even been taught that the Holy Spirit is at work only when we simply trust Him to give us the message of the hour as we walk to the front of the auditorium. If not for the seriousness of this I would laugh myself silly with sarcasm.

A few of us fight the temptation to allow someone else to do the work for us. We can access the sermons of others through all the numerous preaching websites loaded with potential messages. Please, please, please be careful of anything that would short-circuit your own study. All of us borrow from others; there is nothing wrong with that. The problem is we live in a world where it is easy to simply cut and paste a sermon from someone else's study. Scott Gibson is absolutely correct. "Plagiarism is stealing someone else's words or thoughts and claiming them as your own. The Latin root—*plagiaries*—means kidnapper" (*Should We Use Someone Else's Sermon?*, 15). It would be time well spent to read through Gibson's book. He not only explains the problem, but he digs into the ethics of plagiarizing and shows us a way out of the mess. Somewhere I recall Spurgeon suggesting that the preacher who would never use the thought of another man's brain proved that he had no brain of his own! What I am talking about here is the wholesale stealing of someone else's sermon. That kind of conduct should be labeled for what it is—stealing. It is a kind of thievery that harms the soul of the preacher and the congregation. Finally, some preachers, young and old, simply confess that it is the lack of developing and cultivating their own rhythm and habits that has hurt their life of study. All of us need to find a pattern of study that suits our personality and daily pace. None of us are exactly alike. How I would spend my day in study may differ from many other preachers. I am simply calling for a life of study that fits each preacher's unique situation.

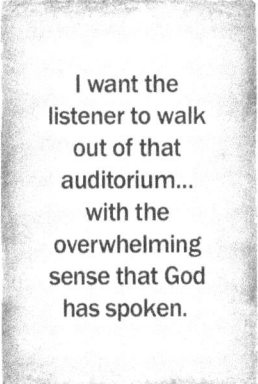

I want the listener to walk out of that auditorium... with the overwhelming sense that God has spoken.

Preachers who want to let the text win over their life of study must find a routine that fits their personality and ministry context. Some suggestions are in order. The influence of Fred Craddock will be evident to those who have read him and appreciated him as much as I have (*Preaching*, 69-83). Dr. Craddock's contribution to my life is inestimable.

1. Create a schedule for study that fits you and then inform the congregation of your commitment to be the best student of the Word that you can be. Most churches will honor that kind of preacher. They know that a preacher who studies regularly and consistently will, in the long run, be a better shepherd and leader. I did this myself nearly thirty years ago and I found, for the most part, that people were respectful and grateful. I was a young preacher overwhelmed by all the responsibilities of located ministry. I prayed, sought counsel, and talked with my secretary. She became my able assistant in helping me to find the best hours for study. I have always been a morning person, and so we decided together that my first hours of the day would be guarded and protected. She grouped my phone calls and commitments so that I could have the morning for concentrated study. The congregation began to hear better sermons and my life began to be larger and fuller because the Word was deeply addressing my own life. Maybe your personality is the opposite and your best study time is in the evening. I would suggest, then, that you structure your day accordingly and explain it to your listeners. Whatever you do, stick to the rhythm of getting into the text early in the week and coming out of the text with a sermon ready to be preached at the end of the week. Fred Craddock is right: "The busy person has no better friend than routine and habit" (*Preaching*, 77).

> All of us need to find a pattern of study that suits our personality and daily pace. None of us are exactly alike.

2. Locate all the best resources at hand that will assist you in your preaching journey. A preacher has no better friend or mentor than his own good library. The development of that library is critically important to the life of study. I know that books and software can be expensive. If I had a magic wand, I would bless every preacher with the software gift of Logos, the Scholar's Edition. Ask those you trust what the best resources are. Not all commentaries are equal. I have tended to avoid purchasing complete sets. Instead, I have obtained the best volumes I could locate. Sometimes that process includes going to garage sales, estate sales, or library closings. Book gifts from preachers who are no longer preaching as much as they did when they were younger can be invaluable. My father gave me numerous volumes

when his health no longer allowed him to preach. Talk to those near you who have developed a good personal library. Get on the mailing list of the major publishing firms and receive their book catalogs. Keep a "wish list" of books that you eventually would like to own. I have been blessed on several occasions by people who simply want to help me build a better library. They have given me birthday and Christmas book gifts. I thank God for their kindness. I have praised my mother-in-law for all that she has done to improve my library (See *Reading with God in Mind*, HeartSpring, 2004). Borrow books. Make sure you return them! Locate the best libraries near you. Pick a few quality journals and magazines and subscribe to them. If you can't afford to do that, go to your nearest public library or seminary and spend a day a month reading. John Stott's example has challenged me greatly. Stott read about six hundred hours a year. He accomplished this amazing feat by reading one hour every day, four hours one day a week, a whole day once a month, and a whole week once a year! Why not join a reading group or create your own? Do everything you can to continue to get your hands on the best resources. Some preachers move from church to church simply because they fail to continue to study. I once heard a very wise preacher say, "Better to buy a book than rent a moving van." He meant that it is cheaper for the minister to invest himself in a good book that will deepen his ministry, than to rent an expensive moving van and start over somewhere else.

> "The busy person has no better friend than routine and habit."

3. Develop a system for saving the good fruit of your study. One of the ways to do this is by setting up your library so that it is usable. By that I mean that you know what you have on the shelf. If for no other reason than insurance purposes, a preacher should know what resources he owns. Organize it so that you have quick access to it. Find a system that fits you. It might be a topical approach. It might be that you use a more formalized system like the Rossin-Dewey Decimal system. This principle also holds true of your files, both the paper kind and the electronic kind. Set it up so that you can quickly and easily retrieve what you need. Files of any kind are not just for storing. Those files are for recovering

what you need when you need it. I keep all of my study notes. Why would I throw away hours of work once the sermon or teaching is completed? Over the course of several decades of study the preacher can develop incredible resources of word studies, background work, and contextual awareness that can save enormous time.

4. Develop the habit of knowing how to take advantage of small units of time. Those of you who are experienced preachers know how cumbersome it is sometimes to locate large blocks of uninterrupted time. Our study often takes place between appointments, interruptions, hospital visits, and drive-time. I have made it a holy habit to take my study with me everywhere I go. I always have a book at hand or the current sermon I'm working on at my side. I have found that fifteen minutes here or thirty minutes there can offer an immense contribution to my life of study. T.D. Jakes was reflecting on how he took advantage of thinking about his sermon text indirectly. He loves studying himself full, thinking himself clear, praying himself hot, and letting himself go. Jakes says,

> My days are rapid pace: often traveling here, there, and everywhere, board meetings, dealing with issues. . . . But in the back of my mind that message is still turning that I had received during the night and it builds, it develops. It's almost like you take a piece of meat and you marinate it for a couple of days before you cook it. I like to marinate a message—sometimes a few days and sometimes a few weeks. I've got messages in my head that have been in the back of my head for months. (*Preaching*, September–October 2003, 43)

I recall a story about Kenneth Taylor, who, like Eugene Peterson of our day, wanted to write a translation or paraphrase of the Bible that would help others, especially his children, understand more clearly the Scriptures. He wrote that wonderful work, *The Living Bible*, while commuting on the train to and from work. He bought up the time that was given to him. Wise preachers understand.

"Better to buy a book than rent a moving van."

5. Don't stop studying once the dominant thought of your sermon surfaces. I have hinted at this back in chapter one. It is so easy to do our little dance, sing our joyful song, and shout out a loud yelp of thanksgiving when we feel that our study has finally revealed the focus of the sermon. We must do all that we can to resist the allure of concluding that our study is over. I know and understand the temptation. I get a weekly headache when my study has not yet revealed to me the sermonic sentence. I so badly want to find the focus of the message that when it reveals itself to me I want to exhale and start crafting the structure. Chapter six will describe in greater detail how the text can win over the sermon in a sentence. For now, it is crucial that all of us grasp what is at stake if we yield to the easy way out. Our sermons will lack the extra muscle and vigor that separates good messages from better ones. I notice in the sermon worksheets that my students sometimes give me that the first half of their study is exceptionally strong, but once they locate the central idea of the message their exploration into the text stops. Keep the sail up. Let the Spirit continue to blow on that message.

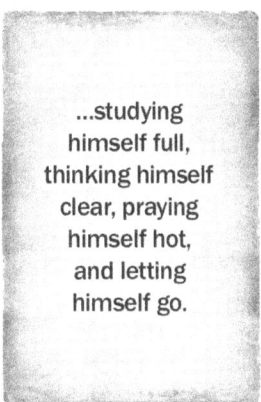

...studying himself full, thinking himself clear, praying himself hot, and letting himself go.

6. Create a methodology that gets you into the rhythm of study each week. I offer my own approach as *a* method, not *the* method. I have a six-step process that suits me. I have passed this along to my students as a way of saying to them, "Create your own." Usually on Monday morning I take what I call the "personal step" into the text. I begin with a posture of humility and prayer. The biblical text is far bigger than I am. I read it aloud and repeatedly. I ask a lot of questions. Where does this speak to my life? How does this comfort and/or confront me? What questions surface for me as a result of my reading this passage? What words catch my attention? What stories, experiences, images, or metaphors surface as I read and reflect? What is the text's dominant thought? My past practice included having several people over to my house to take this first step with me. They helped me "listen." Our approach at Eastview (Normal, IL) is to gather as a preaching team on Monday afternoons. We begin with a word of prayer and then systematically work through the text. Sometimes the

questions I mentioned above get thrown into the conversation. We spend an hour simply helping each other listen to the text. We pray again and then close our time of study. I am indebted to Mike Baker, Charlie Welke, Matt Fogel, and Caleb Baker.

The next step is a Monday or Tuesday step, depending on how much time I have available. I call this step the "cultural step." I try to discover the historical setting of the passage. Again, I ask several key questions. What's going on behind this passage and in this passage? Are there other passages that might help me to understand this one?

Keep the sail up. Let the Spirit continue to blow on that message.

Sometime on Tuesday I take a third step, which I call the "textual step." I take a good look at the boundaries of my passage, making sure that I have a legitimate preaching unit. I read the text again. Often, I will incorporate a variety of translations. I do my original language work in this step as well. I like asking, "What kind of genre am I dealing with here? Does that matter? Can I imitate the mood of this passage as well as the message of this passage? What difference would it make if this passage were not located here?"

On Wednesday I move to my "exegetical step." I love asking, "What does this text mean?" I explore commentaries. I do word studies. I call or email people who might lend me an insight into the text. I take lots of notes. I ask, "How does this passage relate to the other passages that surround it? How does this text relate to the rest of Scripture? How has the church at large understood this text? Can I put the meaning of this passage into a sentence that says what the text is saying with the vocabulary of the passage?"

On Wednesday or Thursday I move to my fifth step. I call this one the "theological step." I spend a lot of time here reflecting and praying. I ask more questions. What does this passage say about God? Where are Jesus Christ and the gospel located? What gives this text weight and size? Where is the "so what" of the text? How does this passage speak to my listeners?

Finally, on Thursday or early Friday I come to my "practical step." I want to put all of my study into one clear, contemporary and concise sentence. So, I will ask, "How can I say this? How can I communicate this in the best manner? What would God have me say? What has the Holy Spirit impressed upon me? What do I want my listeners to know, be, and do based on this text? Should I save my dominant thought to the end, introduce it early, or place it somewhere in the middle of the message?" I begin to structure the message and put flesh on the skeleton. I have been following this simple routine for years. It fits me. Find one that fits you and stick to it.

There remains a large assumption behind the commitment to lifelong study. It is assumed that the preacher not only desires to preach the whole will of God (Acts 20:27), but has discovered the need for planning. A caution is in order. The more gifted the preacher is, the more that preacher needs to study and plan.

Preaching widely and deeply requires a plan. The study life of the preacher has a natural by-product to it. It is the preaching plan that is born out of the preacher's own desire to grow and to help his congregation grow. This plan can come in any size and shape. It is simply a servant, not a task-master. I prefer planning a year in advance. Other preachers prefer the six month approach or even a quarterly approach. What is important is that the preacher realizes that a plan grows out of a life of study. That good plan saves time in the long run. It decreases the weekly "birthing pains" that many preachers feel when they have to locate another text and subject to preach. It also builds the foundation for a solid teaching ministry and it invites the listener to work alongside the preacher. It gives the preacher's thought process the needed time to contemplate, meditate, and incubate on the text. I find that having a good preaching plan keeps me from those favorite themes I spoke of earlier, increases my library, and helps me to gather needed support material, especially illustrations, far in advance. More than anything, I think a good plan simply honors Scripture and focuses the worship service around a particular biblical text. With this in mind, I offer the following example of a yearlong preaching plan that I carried out several years ago. You will notice that my plan has a general theme to guide it, some subthemes to focus it, and all the dates, passages, special

> More than anything, I think a good plan simply honors Scripture and focuses the worship service...

days, and sermon starters or sermon titles that assist the listener to read and think ahead. You will also see a balance between the Old and New Testament. If the one I am proposing does not seem to fit your personality and ministry context take a look at Calvin Miller's example in *Marketplace Preaching*. He offers a splendid model from his own years of preaching (145-168). You can also access another plan in Appendix C.

PREACHING PLAN EXAMPLE
"Discovering What We Have Always Wanted."

Discovering . . . Values Worth Believing (CORE VALUES)

January

2	Ps 46	Created to Worship God
9	Luke 15	Commissioned to Seek Lost People
16	1 Pet 1:13-2:3	Challenged to Grow
23	Luke 12:35-48	Commanded to be Whole-life Stewards
30	Mark 10:35-45	Convinced to Serve

February

6	John 13:34-35	Called to Care

Discovering . . . The Relationship Worth Having (ROMANS)

February

13	Intro to Book	Discovering the Relationship Worth Having
20	1:1-17	Why I'm a Jesus-Follower
27	1:18-32	What Happens When God Has Had Enough

March

6	2:1-16	God Knows Something We Don't
13	2:17-3:8	Why Religion Can't Save Me (Part 1)
20	3:9-20	Sailing First-Class on the Titanic
27 (EASTER)	3:21-4:25	The Trusting-God-to-Do-It Gift

April

3 (MISSIONS)	5:1-6:23	The Pilgrim's Progress
10 (MISSIONS)	7:1-25	When You've Tried Everything and Nothing Helps
17 (MISSIONS)	8:1-39	Too Good to Be False
24 (MISSIONS)	9:1-33	God the Evangelist (PART 1)

May

1 (BABY'S DAY/ PENTECOST)	10:1-21	Why Religion Can't Save Me (PART 2)

8 (MOM'S DAY)	11:1-32	God the Evangelist (PART 2)
15	11:33-36	In-over-My-Head Praise
22 (GRAD'S DAY)	12:1-2	24/7 Worship
29 (MEM. DAY)	12:3-8	The Charismatic Worship Challenge

June

5	12:9-16	Real Worship 101
12	12:17-21	Real Worship 201
19 (DAD'S DAY)	13:1-7	What a Worshiping Citizen Looks Like
26	13:8-10	What an In-debt Worshiper Looks Like

July

3	13:11-14	Staying Awake during Worship
10	14:1-15:13	Getting Along with Other Worshipers
17	15:14-22	Whatever Happened to This Kind of Worship
23	15:23-33	Surrendering Our Plans to the One We Worship
31	16:1-27	Praise God from Whom All Blessings Flow

Discovering . . . The Life Worth Living (Ecclesiastes)

August

7 (VBS)	1:1-11	What 'Been There and Done That' Looks Like
14 (STEWARDSHIP)	1:12-2-26	Experiment in Progress: Whose Beaker Is This?
21 (STEWARDSHIP)	3:1-22	Does Anybody Really Know What Time It Is?
28 (STEWARDSHIP)	4:1-16	What Do I Really Want?

September

4 (LABOR DAY)	5:1-7	"Shhhhh"
11 (FALL KICK-OFF)	5:8-6:12	If I Were a Rich Man
18	7:1-8:1	Who Is the Wise Guy?
25	8:2-17	When 20/20 Isn't Good Enough

October

2	9:1-10:20	Whistling While I Work
9	11:1-12:8	How to Keep Your Faith from Going to Seed
16	12:9-14	The Bottom Line

Discovering . . . Beliefs Worth Valuing (JSCC Beliefs)

October

23	Gen 1:1-2:4A	A God like That
30	Col 1:15-20	The One and Only Jesus

November

6 (BABY DAY)	John 16:5-15	Where the Spirit Goes
13 (VET DAY)	Tim 3:16-17	The Book Worth Everything
20 (THANKS)	Gen 3:1-4:26	Lost and Not Found
27	2 Pet 3:1-18	Room for One More

Discovering . . . Songs Worth Singing (Advent from Luke)

December

4	1:46-55	When I Count My Blessings
11	1:68-79	When I Ponder His Plan
18	2:14	When Peace Is a Possibility
25 (CHRISTMAS)	2:29-32	When My Prayer Is Answered

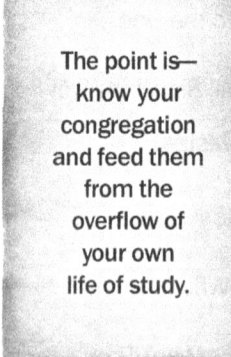

The point is—know your congregation and feed them from the overflow of your own life of study.

Some of you will look at this plan and say, "That would never work in my church." You may be absolutely correct. Some preachers do a specific series of sermons for only three to six weeks. The point is—know your congregation and feed them from the overflow of your own life of study. If my study is to be productive, then I must keep my heart humble. That is formation. The text must win me first! I must keep my eyes open. That is observation. If I watch the text, it will watch me. I must keep my mind engaged. That is interpretation. If I avoid shortcuts that suggest I am only a mouse click away from doing new and easy Bible study, then the text has a chance to win. I must keep my feet on the ground. That is application. Remember that Bible passages come to us from specific times, places, and circumstances. We live in another time, place, and circumstance. When I don't forget that truth, the text has a chance to win. I must keep my knees bent at all times. That is submission, worship, and meditation. The text wins when I stay on my knees.

Let the focus of your study life and your preaching always exalt and elevate Jesus. Blaise Pascal said, "Apart from Jesus Christ we cannot know the meaning of life or of our death, of God or of ourselves. Without Scripture, whose only object is to proclaim Christ, we know nothing, and we can see nothing but obscurity and confusion in the nature of God and in nature itself" (*Mind on* Fire, ed. James Houston, 153). Immerse yourself in prayer and invite God's Word to win over your lifelong commitment of study.

CHAPTER 5
LETTING THE TEXT WIN IN THE STUDY: Part 2 (MS)

Habit is a great liberator. It might seem like a straightjacket, but it is just the opposite. Good habits reap destinies. Solid homiletical habits were identified in the last chapter. In this chapter we want to argue for allowing habit to guide the work of the sermon from the hard chair.[50]

No One Way

There is probably no one way to do the hard chair work of sermon preparation. There might be preferred ways to ensure ascertaining the biblical writer's intention. But there is a danger of creating a legalistic checklist wherein supposed accuracy to the text is thought to come by hermeneutical sweat as opposed to devotional submission to God.

The main thing to remember in sitting down at the hard chair is to carve out sufficient time. This process can't be rushed. Good brisket takes all day to cook. The same is true with sermon preparation. In fact, it takes days (as outlined in the previous chapter). John Killinger reminds us, "Shallow persons preach few deep sermons."[51]

As much as I would love to find a textual variant in the ancient manuscripts telling us how to study the Bible,[52] there really is none to be found. The only method of Bible study recorded in the Bible itself is the constant rereading of the text. This takes time. In the words of the Psalmist, "On his law I meditate day and night" (Ps 1:2). When a new king arose in Israel his job was to write a copy of the law for himself, read it all the days of his life, and follow it carefully (Deut 17:18-20). This takes time.

---

50. Fred B. Craddock, *Preaching* (Nashville: Abingdon, 1985). Craddock develops this idea of the "hard chair" for the serious study of the hermeneutical side of the sermon preparation and the "soft chair" for the homiletical side of the sermon preparation. When this book was published, four segments of his preaching class were filmed that semester at Candler School of Theology (Emory University) to coincide with the book.
51. John Killinger, *Fundamentals of Preaching* (Philadelphia: Fortress, 1985) 188.
52. Things identified in the historical-grammatical method of Bible study such as considering context, words, parallel passages, historical background, and grammar.

The Big Goal

However you go about the hard chair work the goal remains the same. Strive to find out what the biblical writer is really saying. Remember that true interpretation is what the author intended to say. Paradigms of understanding and presuppositions keep us from making this an exact science. But by paying attention to the right things, we can let the text have it's own voice. Warren and David Wiersbe remind us, "A clever outline can be ruined by good exegesis."[53] Far better to ruin an outline than to ruin the truth.

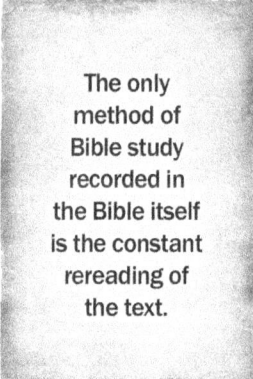

The only method of Bible study recorded in the Bible itself is the constant rereading of the text.

The main purpose in this is simple. Any other approach will cause the preacher to abandon his authority. If we can't find within the Bible something that says what we want to say it is most likely that what we want to say does not have the "ring of truth" and authority of God behind it. Walter C. Kaiser advocated always keeping one finger on the text.[54]

When the text wins, the preacher's study in the hard chair moves him from exegesis/hermeneutics to exposition to application; or from what the text says, to what it means, to how it applies; or from observation to interpretation to application. This is the movement that best protects preachers from saying what the Bible does not say. One preacher of another generation said, "When is the Bible not the Bible? When we make it say what it doesn't say."[55]

Ways to Cut Our Losses

Maybe no method of sermon preparation is actually poor. Any effort at working at the biblical text probably has some redeeming value. But there are some methods to prefer over others, and preachers can cut their losses of running the risk of error if they will pay attention to some basic hermeneutical guidelines. These guidelines are transcultural, and they derive their authority by their common acceptance. They are not handed down by popes or councils. Every tribe, tongue, and nation that

---

53. Warren Wiersbe and David Wiersbe, *The Elements of Preaching* (Wheaton, IL: Tyndale House, 1986) 32.
54. Walter C. Kaiser Jr., Class Notes from Hermeneutics and Homiletics in the Old Testament, Trinity Evangelical Divinity School, summer, 1988. The rest of the statement went, "And if the preacher gets tired then switch fingers and gesture with the other finger."
55. The quote is attributed to Olin Hay.

uses a written script embraces these in one form or another.[56]

The study of the Bible for sermonic work is much larger than Western Christian Civilization. But when authorial intent is jettisoned and all meaning is viewed as indeterminate, the result is hermeneutical chaos where the reader is in total control of the text. Walter Liefeld reminds us, "Given the subjectivity of the preacher, the limitations of the human mind, the effect of subjectivism on modern theology, it is more likely than not that a sermon will contain some error of fact or judgment. Therefore, the closer we stay to God's revealed Word, the less prone we will be to error."[57] There are some ways to ensure staying close to the revealed Word.

In the former chapter JK marked out his study method by the days of the week. He moved from devotion to exegesis/hermeneutics to practicality through the work. The hard chair work was mainly done from Monday afternoon through Thursday morning. Things like finding the preaching unit (textual boundaries), identifying the genre, commentary and word study work, and finally discerning the theology in the passage were all mentioned as hard chair activities. It was our plan to probe some of those steps a bit deeper and add a few other items here.

Five Hard-Chair Steps to Ensure That the Text Wins

The first step to ensure that the text wins is to *secure the text*. It may even seem odd to urge. However, many sermons fly off into the wild blue yonder because they never get attached to a strong text.[58] Aren't all texts good? Yes. Aren't all texts inspired by God? Yes. But the Bible is not flat. Not all verses are created equal. Because the Bible is a story, some parts of the story are more telling about the overall theme than others. And, some texts are heard best on certain days. Many preachers are tempted to avoid the familiar passages. But guess why they are familiar? It's because they are that good. Traditional wedding vows are traditional because they have stood the test of time. There is no reason to embrace

---

56. This might seem like an overstatement, especially to philosophy majors. It also smacks of overconfidence in the historical-grammatical method of Bible study, which might be, to some extent, a product of the Enlightenment. But I would argue that nuances of the historical-grammatical method of Bible study were evident in the Jewish hermeneutics of the first century AD and in the Antioch School in the third and fourth century AD long before the Enlightenment.
57. Walter L. Liefeld, *New Testament Exposition* (Grand Rapids: Zondervan, 1984) 7.
58. This sounded so strange to me years ago. Dr. Wayne Shaw suggested in Advanced Preaching Class (Fall, 1976) that the first step to a good sermon was to get a good text. In my preaching youthfulness I figured that if the text was in the Bible it was already a good text. However, having brought in some texts kicking and screaming in my early years of preaching I found how sound the advice was.

a novel text or some hidden passage just to be unique.[59]

The second step to ensure that the text wins is to *determine the text*. At first hearing this sounds like the same thing as secure the text, but it is not. This step can further refine the choice of the text from the first step. In the last chapter JK spoke about the "preaching unit" and finding the "boundaries" of the text. This is what we mean here. Maybe additional hard chair work will demand expanding the text you secured. Maybe it will shrink. The preacher should ask, "What would be missing in this overall context if I removed this text?" Following the plot or argument really matters for determining the text. Transitional terms (e.g., therefore, in order that, but, etc.) all matter in determining the text.

When we suggest that preachers should determine the text we don't mean that the preacher has to allow that whole text to be the preaching text. For instance, let's suppose that the preacher wants to preach on the descent of the Holy Spirit on the household of Cornelius (The Gentile Pentecost). The text is Acts 10:44-48. There is plenty in that short paragraph to expose. But the preacher would want to determine the text to find its perimeters. Additional study shows that the text really begins in Acts 10:1 and doesn't conclude until Acts 11:18. Awareness of that greatly aids the interpretive and homiletical process.

> ...preachers can cut their losses of running the risk of error if they will pay attention to some basic hermeneutical guidelines.

The third step to ensure that the text wins is to *establish the text*. This might sound like a step reserved only for the critical scholars, but preachers also need to pay attention. We are speaking of the science known as textual criticism and handling textual variants. Can the preacher really know what the text actually says? Perhaps the preacher doesn't have fine-tuned linguistic skills or the knowledge of ancient manuscripts. It is after all a technical aspect of the hard chair work. However, newer and multiple translations and good available tools make this task easier today.[60]

Here is why it matters. I was preaching once from Matthew 18:15-20. This is the familiar passage usually labeled, "church discipline." It

---

59. This is not to say there aren't some "diamonds in the rough" passages still to be found. Neither is it to say that preachers shouldn't, from time to time, preach on obscure passages. People do need to know all the council of God (Acts 20:27). But it is to say that some obscure passages get such press that they take on a life of their own (e.g. the prayer of Jabez in 1 Chr 4:9-10).
60. Bruce Metzger, *A Textual Commentary on the Greek New Testament*, 2nd ed. (New York: American Bible Society, 1994) is in English and very readable. This is also available in various Bible software packages today.

is part of Jesus' fourth discourse in the Gospel. I preached the sermon only to be met in the foyer by a lady who announced, "Your Bible is different from mine." I said, "How so?" She said, "Well, when you read the text you read, 'When you brother sins . . .'" She went on, "My Bible says, 'When your brother sins *against you.*'" She continued, "Doesn't the *against you* change the meaning of who and when we are to confront?" Busted! The preacher may not need to become a Bruce Metzger (a textual criticism expert), but he or she can do as much as possible with the tools available to establish the real text.

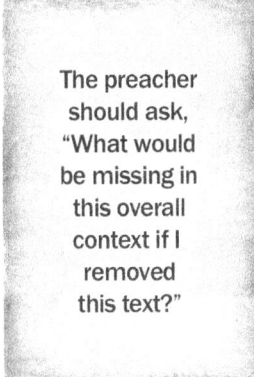

The preacher should ask, "What would be missing in this overall context if I removed this text?"

The fourth step to ensure that the text wins is *identify the text.* This means more than just calling it out (e.g., "My text today is . . ."). It means that the preacher can label the text's genre and subgenre. This simple step can make all the difference in how the text will be preached.[61] This labeling helps the preacher to know what the text says but also *how* it says it.[62] This is not only responsible but also courteous.

It is one thing to preach *from* the text. This means that the preacher derives the homiletical substance from the Scripture and not somewhere else. In other words the sermon says what the text really says. It is another thing to preach *through* the text. This means the preacher moves chronologically or selectively through a Bible book in some kind of systematic way. The preacher is giving high regard to the literary and historical context. However, it is quite another thing to preach *like* the text. This is genre awareness. This is the ability to regard both the content and method of the text.

Being aware of a text's genre sets expectations and guides the hermeneutical constructs. If I say, "These three guys went into a bar . . . ," the listener knows that he or she is about to hear a joke. If I say, "Roses are red; violets are blue . . . ," the listener knows that he or she is going to hear poetry. If I say, "The party of the first part addresses the party of the second part . . . ," the listener knows that he or she is going to hear some kind of legal jargon. Labeling the genre sets the hermeneutical grid for

---

61. Later in the chapter we will identify the major concerns with each of the Bible's main types of literature.
62. Fred Craddock reminds us that the text had already been shaped. It's already been preached. See Fred B. Craddock, "The Sermon and the Text," Seventeenth Annual Spring Lectureship, Lincoln Christian Seminary, May 7-8, 1985.

how to interpret the next lines. Labeling the genre helps us ask proper questions of the text.

Identifying the text helps us know with what kind of text we are dealing. Is it narrative? Poetic? Prophetic? Parabolic? Epistolary? Apocalyptic? I like also to ask about the subgenre of the text. The macro genre (large picture) helps most with hermeneutics. The micro (or sub) genre (smaller picture) helps most with the homiletics. For instance, in the text where Jesus miraculously calms the sea (Mark 4:35-41) the macro genre is Gospel narrative. It is a story. But the subgenre is interrogative. Three questions are asked in the narrative. They are: "Do you not care that we are perishing?" (disciples), "How is it that you have no faith?" (Jesus), "Who then is this that even the winds and waves obey him?" (disciples). Not only can the subgenre provide a possible structure for the sermon, it informs the dominant thought as well.[63]

So probe deeper than just large picture genre. Also ask: Is the text descriptive? Didactic? Indicative? Imperative? Example? Two more examples will illustrate what we are saying. People of our religious heritage have often used Acts 20:7 as the key verse for the frequency of the Lord's Supper. It does say that on the *first day of the week* the church at Troas met together *to break bread*. Clearly this is a purpose clause in Greek. A major purpose for them coming together was to observe the Lord's Table. But where is the imperative? The text is narrative.[64]

Another example would be Psalm 51:5. Nathan has just left the Jerusalem Oval Office. David lies in a heap on the floor facing his sin. He cries out for the mercy of God. He feels so bad for what he has done that he says that his mother must have conceived him in sin. A proof text for the doctrine of original sin? Perhaps. Or could it be a strong example of poetic exaggeration? He feels, after all, lower than a snake's belly. While Bible doctrine can come via the hymnal (Psalms) and stories (parables), be careful here. Allow genre at its macro and micro levels to assist in the hard chair work.

The fifth step to ensure that the text wins is *locate the text*. By locate I don't mean "find it in the Bible." That has been done long ago. I mean

---

63. A dominant thought (big idea) might sound like this, "All of questions of faith disappear when we focus on the object of our faith."
64. This is not to say that there can be no implied imperatives from narrative texts. If the context makes it clear that the biblical writer is setting up the example with approval and if the example is commanded elsewhere in the Bible, one could build a good case for suggesting that an approved precedent is being presented. However, even then, let's be consistent. The rest of the verse says that Paul preached until midnight. Who is ready for that? Evidently not Eutychus.

locate it in all of its categories—linguistically, historically, culturally, socially, theologically, and ecclesiastically. This is clearly hard chair work. And, not all of the categories are equal in significance.

I will comment briefly on the first four categories and expand on the last two. By locating the text linguistically I mean pay the price of the language element. Even if the preacher's skills in the original languages are not strong, commentary work and Bible software can be tremendous aids. Historical background, while being extremely interesting, has to be watched carefully. I have witnessed in preaching too often the background becoming the foreground. Cultural issues and social issues of the biblical world must also be watched for exaggerated use, but certain things in a shame/honor culture like in the Middle East are not our default settings and therefore must be studied. Be sure the text continues to win and not the background.

I especially want to draw a bead on locating the text theologically and ecclesiastically. The reason for this emphasis is that more often than not these two categories are all but neglected. If the text is to win, then each petite text must fit into the metanarrative. This has been the major problem in my own preaching and the preaching I have heard for years. Lots of good things can be preached from the Bible. Many of them are helpful to daily life and live close to the ground, where the best application always resides. However, how does the little story fit into God's massive story? Unless this work of locating the text theologically is done the message becomes quite anthropocentric. If the preacher just preaches on Abraham's good qualities (and he had several bad ones too), then the preacher might as well preach on Abraham Lincoln. He was a good guy too. As much as I need and enjoy sermons on leadership from Nehemiah, or sermons on how to be a better husband from the Song of Songs (I'm turning red), or sermons on expanding my influence and witness (e.g., the prayer of Jabez), I must ask, "Where does this locate itself in the divine story?" How does my text reveal God's plan to save the world through Jesus and heal all of creation as it moves us to new creation? Unless I get that question asked and answered, I might as well give my *talk* to the local Kiwanis Club. While a sermon does not have to be a display of exegesis or theology, it should be at the service

> It is one thing to preach *from* the text. It is another thing to preach *through* the text.

of the redemptive purposes of God in universe.

This is also true about ecclesiology. The audience of worship might be God, but the audience of the message is God's people.[65] God doesn't need a sermon. He wrote the book. A preacher who wants to let the text win will always ask, "What is the meaning of the text for Israel and the church?" Of course part of the hard chair work is sifting through intended audiences to ascertain the proper and keen (i.e., not generic) application. Locate the text with God's plan and God's people.

Context, Content, and Intent

If the text is to win in the sermon the dominant accent of preaching will be expositional. This is not to say that there aren't other valid ways to preach (e.g., topical presentations, analogical presentations, etc.). It is just to say that if a preacher will make exposition his or her primary style of preaching, over the long haul of ministry the Bible will be heard. And *the how* exposition can have a variety of looks as chapter seven will demonstrate.

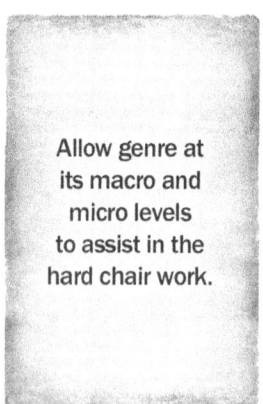

Allow genre at its macro and micro levels to assist in the hard chair work.

But what identifies that exposition? For years, as a hobby, I collected definitions of expository preaching.[66] The sky is the limit on those definitions. Some define exposition by doctrine stating how exposition comes from God. Others define it by length stating how it deals with a "substantial" portion of Scripture (i.e., not a small passage). Others define it by homiletical strategy by showing how the points and subpoints come directly from the text. Still others define it by definition, by suggesting that the sermon exposes the text. While I enjoyed reading and appreciating various nuances of those definitions of expositional preaching, they all left me flat. Of course exposition means to explain, and it gets God a hearing, but we are not asking about its definition or its source. We are asking, whether long text or short, what

---

65. It is beyond the scope of this book to discuss the place of the "seeker" in the Christian assembly (cf. 1 Cor 14:24-25). From the earliest days unbelievers attended believer assemblies just as crowds and multitudes hung around Jesus and the disciples. It is one thing to use the language of the customer and put the cookies where everyone can reach them. It is another thing to design the whole service around the outsiders and decide to do evangelism at "church." That's a judgment that each congregation has to make. Please be culturally astute enough to admit, however, that the seeker today is vastly different than twenty-five years ago.

66. I know, I have to get out more. But the collection of those definitions on the handout was substantial. It was six pages long, single-spaced.

marks it out as expositional?

I would like to emphasize three primary characteristics. If the hard-chair work can nail down these characteristics I believe the preacher has an expository sermon on his hands. The first of those is *context*. Of course the English word, "context," comes from the Latin word, "contextus," or, "contexere." It means, "woven together." Paying attention to the context will help ensure an expository sermon. Of course there really are context*s* (literary, historical, canonical, covenantal, theological, etc.). All of those contexts are worthy of study in any given sermon. But I have primarily in mind the literary context. To expose a text means that the preacher has traced the plot if the genre is narrative and has traced the argument if the text is epistolary. Due to chapter and verse divisions of our Bible this is often neglected. We operate rather piecemeal when it comes to reading holistically.

A classic example of this is in Walter Liefeld's book, *New Testament Exposition*.[67] He gives examples from four preachers (Preachers Brown, Gray, Green, and White). While each of the preachers said some true things from their texts, only Preacher White was truly expositional because he gave great regard to the literary context. That is to say, he kept his text, which he was exposing, in the flow of the literary context.

I am persuaded this is a key. As a preacher, one fear I have is getting to heaven and running into Peter or Paul. After asking for their autograph, I imagine one of them saying, "Remember that sermon you preached from that passage I wrote? It was a really cool sermon. I was quite engaged. It wasn't at all what I was saying, but it was neat." Ouch. I stand a much better chance of gaining their approval if I keep what I say within the biblical writer's contextual parameters. Someone wisely said that a text without its context is a pretext.

> I must ask...
> How does my text reveal God's plan to save the world through Jesus and heal all of creation as it moves us to new creation?

The second characteristic is *content*. The sermon will be expositional if it declares what is there. Now there are many ways to skin this cat and declare a text's contents (see chapter seven). But somewhere the message must be sure that it teaches that particular content of the passage. It is so easy to just *use* a text as opposed to really teaching its contents. Points don't matter. Subpoints don't

---

67. Liefeld, *New Testament Exposition*, 3-5.

matter. Moves don't matter. What matters is that the biblical substance of that text gets taught.

To do this well we need the power of restraint. The temptation is to say a few things about our primary text and then run off to other texts that are parallel or say it differently or better. If another text says it better, why not just go there? Suppose the chosen text is Genesis 13:1-18. This is the story of Abram's separation from his nephew, Lot. There are several good things to preach in this chapter. One could preach that God blesses us when we obey him (2). One could preach on the importance of worship as Abram built an altar and called on the name of the Lord (4, 18). One could preach against quarreling because of the conflict that it creates (7). One could preach on unity because Abram reminded Lot that they should not quarrel because they were brothers (8). One could preach a sermon on being generous as Abram allows Lot to choose the best land first (9). One could preach on greediness because Lot wanted the richest of ground (10). One could preach against immorality because the people of Sodom and Gomorrah were very wicked (13).

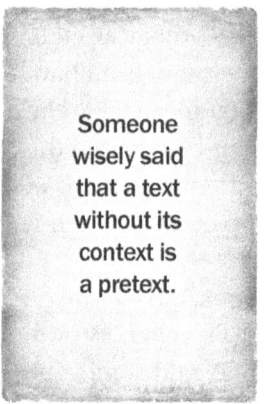

Someone wisely said that a text without its context is a pretext.

There is plenty of homiletical fodder in the above text and paragraph. But what would be the best expositional choice? Where can the text really win? Using the first characteristic of *context* we would back up into Genesis 12 and start reading the story of Abram. We notice that God has a plan to bless Abram and bless the world through him. He was also to leave his family. But Lot hung on. We need to ditch him.[68] So what's the best way to bring in the context and teach the content of the whole chapter? Maybe with a theme such as, "When the Plan of God Stands or Falls with You." This emphasis might also pick up the theological dimension. We must get Abram alone so God can work his plan in the world. Abram walks back and forth in the land[69] among the Canaanites and Perizzites. Those were pagan peoples. What happens when God's plan to save the world through Christ stands or falls with you? That's a larger theme in which the smaller themes

---

68. Of course the latter part of Genesis 12 tells of Abram coming to Canaan and finding a famine. He goes into Egypt to feed his family. Before it's over, he comes out of Egypt with the spoils of Egypt. Sound familiar? In Abram's story is the story of Israel, i.e., God bringing his people out of exile.
69. The Hebrew verb stem is reflexive indicating his back and forth movement throughout the land.

are allowed to fit. The other nuances could be picked up almost as sidebars, but exposition demands paying attention to context and content.

The final characteristic to ensure exposition is *intent*. biblical texts were not just written to inform but to transform. These texts are intended to do something, to accomplish something. Basic to the word "word" in both testaments is this idea of an event or happening. The word is to effect change. The exposition is not complete until the study in the hard chair reveals this. Brother Seth Wilson (longtime academic dean emeritus at Ozark Christian College in Joplin, Missouri) said, "It's one to thing to preach on repentance in such a way for people to understand; it's another thing to preach on it in such a way to where people want to do it."[70]

To put it simply if the text stirs fear, preach in such a way that people scream. If the text stirs joy, preach in such a way that people rejoice. If the text stirs courage, preach in such a way that the people will march seven times around Jericho. If the text stirs shame, preach in such a way that people will turn red on the inside and out. To go where the text goes and be truly expositional means to know *what* it says and *where* it says it, and to *do* what it says to do. Regardless of length or method, that is biblical exposition.

Paying Attention to Primary Old and New Testament Genre to Ensure That the Text Wins

If the history of biblical scholarship in the West reveals anything, it surely reveals that scholarship bounces around and swings back and forth. There is much point and counterpoint. With the embrace of reason as supreme in the Enlightenment came destructive higher criticism with all of its questions and doubts. The questions forced the church (and preachers) to the hard chair, and the doubts created new questions. This was not all bad. Hard sciences like biblical archaeology and textual criticism helped provide answers for tough destructive higher critical theories.

But when the text's historicity was established again then came the hermeneutical debate. How should we interpret these texts? Someone said, "Interpretation used to be so easy, and then someone called it hermeneutics." What surfaced after the more stiff analysis of the text with word studies, grammatical findings, parallel passages, etc. was the whole world of rhetoric. Thus, genre: a French term meaning "type of literature." I have a hard time thinking of a major evangelical book on Bible interpretation within the last 15-20 years where there is not a heavy accent

---

70. Seth Wilson, "Life of Christ" Class Notes, Ozark Christian College, Fall, 1973.

on how to interpret in light of a text's genre.⁷¹ Perhaps the larger challenge for Christians today does not spring from the science department but from the literature department. Truth can come to us through many types of literature. But does the truth change depending on how it is wrapped? Preachers need not fear this. In fact, it can not only be exciting for what hermeneutical insights can be gained, but it can also stir the homiletical juices of the preachers. So we turn to the seven major genres of the Bible and ask what should be noted when preparing sermons so the text can win. What interpretive and rhetorical tips can we give?

OT: Narrative

Of course the story of the Bible is just that, a story. Narrative is not only the beginning genre of the Bible, it is the major genre of the Bible. An old rabbinic saying had it, "God created man because he loved stories." And the stories are very selective. Clearly the accent is on God putting into place a plan to get his creation back. History is not the same as story. While the Bible assumes its history, it is selective history.⁷²

> Seth Wilson said, "It's one thing to preach on repentence... it's another thing to preach on it in such a way to where people want to do it."

This story operates on three levels.⁷³ The bottom level is what might be termed the moral or individual level. This is the basic plot line, e.g., David killed Goliath. "Yay," the underdog won. The middle level is the national level. What did the story mean to Israel? Who cares that the little guy won? Well, if he is the next king of Israel it matters since Saul went AWOL. Finally the top level is the cosmic level. It is God's part of the story. How does the story of a shepherd king fit inside God's plan to save the world through Christ? Does it have to do with

---

71. This would have to also include whole sections devoted to "figures of speech in the Bible." Some major works are the following: Gerald Bray, *Biblical Interpretation: Past and Present* (Downers Grove, IL: InterVarsity, 1996); Peter Cotterell and Max Turner, *Linguistics and Biblical Interpretation* (Downers Grove, IL: InterVarsity, 1989); John B. Gabel and Charles B. Wheeler, *The Bible as Literature: An Introduction*, 2nd ed. (New York: Oxford, 1986); Walter C. Kaiser Jr. and Moises Silva, *An Introduction to Biblical Hermeneutics: The Search for Meaning* (Grand Rapids: Zondervan, 1994); William W. Klein, Craig L. Blomberg, and Robert L. Hubbard Jr., *Introduction to Biblical Interpretation* (Dallas: Word, 1993); Dan McCartney and Charles Clayton, *Let the Reader Understand: A Guide to Interpreting and Applying the Bible* (Wheaton, IL: Bridgepoint Books, 1994); A. Berkeley Michelsen, *Interpreting the Bible* (Grand Rapids:. Eerdmans, 1963); Roy Zuck, *Basic Bible Interpretation: A Practical Guide to Discovering Biblical Truth* (Wheaton, IL: Victor Books, 1991).
72. My friend Matt Proctor, president at Ozark Christian College, has observed that Pharaoh's real name is never given in the biblical account. But two Hebrew midwives are named: Shiphrah and Puah. If one was simply recounting history would those be the names that would make a book?
73. Gordon D. Fee and Douglas Stuart, *How to Read the Bible for All Its Worth: A Guide to Understanding the Bible*, 2nd ed. (Grand Rapids: Zondervan, 1993) 79-81.

keeping the name of God honored in the world long enough to get Jesus here through that special seed? There might be limits to Fee and Stuart's three levels of Hebrew narrative. But if preachers would pay attention to those levels it would deliver their preaching from the danger of anthropocentricism. Don't allegorize Goliath. Leave him a nine-foot, two-inch giant. Find the application somewhere other than defeating the various giants in our lives.

Besides recognizing these levels of narrative, what other tips should preachers follow so as to let the narrative text win?

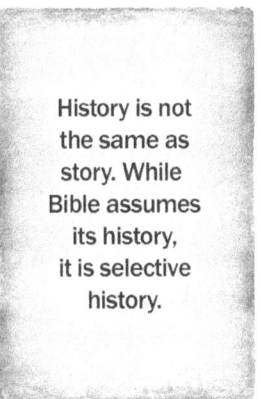

History is not the same as story. While Bible assumes its history, it is selective history.

1. Strive to discern the overall plot. Where does the story begin and how does it end?

2. How many scenes are there to the story and how are they divided?

3. Who are the main characters and what do their names mean? Remember that God is the hero of all the characters.

4. What kind of dialog is taking place? Watch especially paronomasia (play on words).

5. Is there significance to the names of places and events?

6. Are there any significant rhetorical patterns (e.g., repetition, inclusio, chiasm)?

7. What about the two Hebrew ways of humor (irony and sarcasm)?

8. Narrators may not sit in judgment on the narrative. In other words we are not always told by the narrator of a story how we are to feel about that story. The story of David's sin with Bathsheba is an exception (2 Sam 11:27). Reporting the story does not equal agreement with the story (e.g., Abraham's lie about Sarah (Gen 12:10-20).

Answering these questions will not only aid the hermeneutical task, but answering them will also start churning the homiletical butter. While scenes can outline a narrative, strive not to lose the narrative feel as the sermon is developed. We don't tell stories by saying, "Point One."

OT: Legal

Daniel Block refers to legal genre as "constitutional literature."[74] Legal genre consisted of the agreement (i.e., covenant) that God had with Israel. The Torah was given to Israel within a narrative framework of God's redemptive activity. So grace (the exodus) precedes any stipulations. Preachers must remember this or their sermon series on the Ten Commandments will go belly up at the beginning.

As strange as it sounds to us today, Israel had great respect for legal genre. It was partly how the Israelites knew that they belonged to God (besides circumcision and their diet). The psalmists praised the law (Psalm 19; 119), and the prophets explained the intent behind it. Here are some tips to studying and preaching from the legal genre of the Old Testament:

> While scenes can outline a narrative, strive not to lose the narrative feel as the sermon is developed.

1. No Jewish person would have equated law with legalism. So get over that now. The Old Testament is different from Judaism.

2. New Testament writers viewed the law in different ways. Jesus said he came to fulfill it and that it continues *in some way* (Matt 5:17-20). Paul believes that the law is good (Rom 7:12), that Christ and the law are interrelated (Rom. 10:4), that the law can't make a person right with God (Gal 2:16), and that the law leads people to Christ (Gal 3:24). The Hebrew writer says that the law is only a shadow of the good things to come (Heb 10:1).

3. Legal genre has three parts—precept, principle, and person. (This might even be a homiletical pattern to preach some of the legal genre.) First comes the *precept*, "Thou shalt not steal." But what is the *principle* behind that command? Isn't it that God desires that his people be givers and not takers? Finally who is the *person* behind such a command? It is God himself. God is a giver. The legal genre of the Old Testament is a statement about the character and person of God.

4. Legal genre has no division between sacred and secular. This compartmentalization is Western in orientation. Divisions such

---

74. Daniel Block, "Christian Living and Teaching of Old Testament Law," Professional Growth Seminar, sponsored by *Ministry Magazine*, April 2005.

as physical, spiritual, ceremonial, moral, and civil are all imposed categories on the text. The legal genre could in one breath say don't steal (moral) and in the next breath say don't boil a kid in it's mother's milk (cultic). To our forefathers those were just laws from God. Their six categories were clearly different from ours.

5. Legal genre can be preached by using the two umbrella commands of the Old Testament. The Shema (Deuteronomy 6) and the Code of Holiness (Leviticus 18–19) frame up the two greatest commands in all of the Bible. Love God and love neighbor. When preachers are at a loss about how to preach some of the legal genres, they should allow these two broad sweeps to help them out. Does the command help people to love God or people?

6. Legal genre can create a database of understanding for the New Testament. "The holiness of God is a huge theological theme that runs throughout the Old Testament law, and it can be somewhat easily translated into a contemporary Christian setting."[75] We must remember that the "Old Testament law is still the Word of God for us even though it is not still the command of God to us."[76]

7. Legal genre can be used to bring about conviction of sin and address issues of social justice. Rightly principalized this can be a good use of this genre.

One final thought about legal genre is the way Jesus used it when in battle with the enemy (Matt 4:1-11). Legal genre doesn't mess around. When Jesus was tempted to satisfy himself by turning stones into bread, he didn't say, "Devil, let me tell you a story." The abruptness and curtness of this genre serves a noble purpose.

OT: Poetry

Poetry is found throughout the Bible—not just in sections of the Bible. There may be a philosophical reason for this. "As the soul is caught up in the wonder of God the language always approaches that of poetry."[77] How else can we speak of God? Perhaps only in metaphor or viewing language as metaphor.

---

75. Terry G. Carter, J. Scott Duvall, and J. Daniel Hays, *Preaching God's Word: A Hands-On Approach to Preparing, Developing, and Delivering the Sermon* (Grand Rapids: Zondervan, 2005) 244.
76. Fee and Stuart, *How to Read the Bible for All Its Worth*, 153.
77. Seth Wilson, Ozark Christian College Class Notes, Fall, 1975.

A captivating book in this regard is Walter Brueggemann's, *Finally Comes the Poet*.[78] Besides being a fine book on preaching, the book finds its title in a poem from Walt Whitman. After the captains, engineers, inventors, scientists, chemists, geologists, and ethnologists have done all they can do then finally comes the poet. In the poem the poet is "the true son of God." Here are some tips for studying and preaching the poetic genre of the Bible:

> When Jesus was tempted to satisfy himself by turning stones into bread, he didn't say, "Devil, let me tell you a story."

1. Poetic genre is intense. The language of poetry is not for the faint of heart.
   This must be remembered especially when dealing with the imprecatory psalms. When the Psalmist calls down God's wrath on his or her enemies (Dash their children against the rocks? Ps 137:9), preachers must remind themselves that venting to God in poetic verse is one thing while forming one's own vigilante group to take out one's enemy is quite something else. Poetic genre is emotional.

2. Poetic genre plays the comparison game. Simile and metaphor are plastered all over the poetic genre. But parallelism is the main type of comparison. There are a plethora of types of parallelism (e.g., "additional" as seen in Ps 95:1 and "antithetical" as seen in Ps 1:6).

3. Poetic genre uses many other rhetorical devices. Prominent among these would be inclusio, hyperbole, and metonymy. Knowledge of how those tropes are used keeps the preacher from making points out of overly similar ideas.

4. Poetic genre can come to us via lament, thanksgiving, salvation history, royalty, wisdom, and a host of other emphases. Strive to capture not only the content but also the music of the poetry.

OT: Prophetic

If the narrative genre stirs the imagination, the legal genre confronts the will, and the poetic genre engages the heart, then the prophetic genre

---

78. Walter Brueggemann, *Finally Comes the Poet: Daring Speech for Proclamation* (Minneapolis: Fortress, 1989).

scores a direct hit on the conscience. The only way to take the bulk of the prophetic literature is right in the belly. "Prophets are not interested in homiletical 'how to's' nor do they care about style and preparation. Prophets don't prepare messages. Prophets are messages."[79] This type of genre is very aggressive.

There is a sense in which prophetic genre describes the whole Bible (2 Pet 1:20-21). But usually we mean the books of the five major prophets and of the twelve minor prophets.[80] The prophets were more than preachers, but they did preach. They did more forthtelling than foretelling. They were inspired covenant messengers sent from God. They called God's people back to their covenant responsibility. They functioned much like prosecuting attorneys. They were like mean junkyard dogs nipping at the heels of God's people to help them live out Deuteronomy. They gave guidance to kings (the government) and the Levites (education). Here are some tips when studying from and preaching the prophets:

1. Their lives are inextricably linked with their messengers. A caution about biographical preaching is justified.[81] We don't want to forget about God as hero. On the other hand what happened to Israel functions as examples to us (1 Cor 10:11). So there must be some legitimate biographical preaching from the Bible. And the prophets may provide the best example of such. When preaching on the life story of Hosea, one might be really preaching the unrelenting love of God. When preaching on the life story of Jonah, one might be really preaching on the amazing grace of God. When preaching on the life story of Habakkuk, one might really be preaching on the incalculable plan of God.

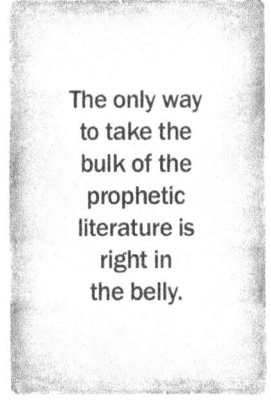

The only way to take the bulk of the prophetic literature is right in the belly.

2. Their *predictive* prophecies are ambiguous, short, and

---

79. Calvin Miller, *Spirit, Word, and Story: A Philosophy of Preaching* (Dallas: Word, 1989) 59.
80. Those divisions are arbitrary. The Jewish division of the prophets was much different. The former prophets were Joshua, Judges, Samuel, and Kings. The latter prophets were Isaiah, Jeremiah, Ezekiel, and the twelve. Daniel was listed in the Writings.
81. See books by Sidney Greidanus such as, *The Modern Preacher and the Ancient Text* (Grand Rapids: Eerdmans, 1988) and *Preaching Christ from the Old Testament* (Grand Rapids: Eerdmans, 1999).

fragmentary. Predictive prophecies differ in their fullness and clarity. Predictive prophecy can be seen with 20/20 vision—after the fulfillment. Some predictive prophecies are fulfilled literally, some are fulfilled figuratively, and some are fulfilled typologically. Allow Old Testament prophecies to be seen as fulfilled in the first coming of Christ as one's default setting. Extend fulfillments only to the second coming of Christ if the text and context make it abundantly clear. Look for timely fulfillment in history.

3. Strive to read the prophecies on their own terms. Ask what would be the natural way the original audience would have understand the prophecy? Make sure to get the major points more than all the symbolic details.

4. Keep in mind *prophetic perspective*. This is called by several other names.[82] It is the idea that things predicted in the long-term future may actually look close to other fulfillments more quickly fulfilled. For instance the destruction of Jerusalem may look close to the return of Christ, but the events are separated by thousands of years.

5. Pay attention to the literary grandeur of the prophets. Reach back to preaching tips on how to study and preach the poetic books and read again the peculiar characteristics of the poetic genre. For instance, in the little prophetic book of Habakkuk (three chapters) there are no less than 46 figures of speech or metaphors.

6. Watch for special nuances of grammar and various rhetorical devices. The prophets can speak of the future as if it has already happened. This is due to the prophet's assurance of the sovereignty of God. With God the future is as good as done. Also hymns, liturgies, woes, and dirges are all tools in the prophet's work belt.

7. Discern the difference between the conditional and unconditional *predictive* prophecies. Sometimes a prophecy is given but its fulfillment is based on whether there will be repentance. If God's people repent, then there may be no need for judgment. For instance, Jonah told the people of Nineveh

---

82. It is called near-far fulfillment, multiple reference, partial reference, progressive reference-fulfillment, split reference, shortened perspective, and double emphasis.

to repent or they would be destroyed. But that judgment never was fulfilled because the 120,000 Ninevites (plus much cattle) repented at the preaching of Jonah.[83]

8. Remember Jesus Christ (cf. 2 Tim 2:8). Don't marginalize Jesus in the prophetic genre. We don't need to allegorize the text to find him there. But we do need to remember, "that the entire story of the prophets, beginning with the death of Moses, is in search of another 'prophet like Moses.' This role is fulfilled by Jesus."[84]

Sometimes we are as dumb as a box of hammers. We need a fountain of smart.

9. Everything has to do with exile. Perhaps the great scholar N.T. Wright over stresses this (i.e., seeing "exile" under every rock). But Israel is always coming out of exile (Exodus) or going back into exile (Babylon). This exile theme is huge with the prophets. Pay attention to it. It is also tied to their genuine, hypocritical, or legalistic worship.

OT: Wisdom

Wisdom genre is everywhere (think bumper stickers). I saw one the other day as I pulled up behind a car. It read, "Honk if you love Jesus. Text while you drive, and you'll meet him."[85] The Bible is filled with wisdom genre—beyond that from Proverbs, Ecclesiastes, and Song of Songs. Sometimes we are as dumb as a box of hammers. We need a fountain of smart. Here are some tips when studying from and preaching from the wisdom genre:

1. Look underneath the text for the theology. At first pass wisdom literature seems like an appendage to the metanarrative of

---

83. However, 100 years later the city was destroyed under the preaching of the prophet Nahum.
84. Leland Ryken, James C. Wilhoit, and Tremper Longman III, *Dictionary of Biblical Imagery* (Downers Grove, IL: InterVarsity, 1998) 674.
85. We sometimes forget how prominent these kinds of statements are. A first-grade school teacher in Virginia had her classroom finish the second half of some secular proverbs. Here are some of the results: Strike while the . . . bug is close. Never underestimate the power of . . . termites. Don't bite the hand that . . . looks dirty. You can't teach an old dog new . . . math. The pen is mightier than the . . . pigs. Happy is the bride who . . . gets all the presents. Children should be seen and not . . . spanked or grounded. Robert Fulghum's book, *All I Ever Needed to Know I Learned in Kindergarten* became a # 1 best seller. Why? I saw the following title in an airport, *Don't Squat with Your Spurs On*. And how do we explain the great popularity of the *Chicken Soup for the Soul* books?

the Bible. But the proverb only needs pulled back to reveal the theology. Some wisdom genre underlines humankind's fallenness. Some wisdom genre underlines God's sovereignty over humankind's efforts to play God. And remember that in Christ are hidden all the treasures of wisdom and knowledge (Col 2:3). You can never separate the fear of the Lord (Prov 1:7) from the practical advice being given.

2. Think of a story that could lie behind the wisdom genre. Someone said, "Proverbs are short sentences drawn from long experiences." For instance, when preaching from Proverbs 5 or 7 about the adulterous woman, a preacher might want to expose 2 Samuel 11 (as well as Psalm 51 and Psalm 32).

3. Remember that wisdom genre doesn't argue; it assumes. Proverbs in particular are short pithy statements of general truth. They aren't intended to handle all the exceptions in life. They are true in their particular settings and context. For instance, Proverbs 22:6 is not a blanket guarantee to reward unblemished parenting but an appeal to do our best with our children. The classic example of this is in Proverbs 26:4 and 26:5. These verses couldn't get any closer. The first ones says, "Do not answer a fool according to his folly . . ." The second one says, "Answer a fool according to his folly." Excuse me? Wisdom is context-specific.

4. Watch for wisdom genre's literary devices. Wisdom genre employs such devises as rhyme, paronomasia, acrostic, puns, alliteration, parallelism, repetition, paradox, and figurative language.

5. Wisdom genre portrays the ideal character of a citizen of the messianic kingdom. This person walks in love, light, and wisdom. Probe the secret of his inner life.

NT: Gospel

The word "gospel" is easy to define (good news). But gospel genre is much more involved. C.F. Evans asked the right question, "If a librarian in Alexandria, Egypt, got a copy of the Gospel of Mark, where would she shelve it?" Evans' answer is that the librarian would have to build a new shelf.

> While the Gospels were written to specific audiences, the writers themselves put the words and deeds of Jesus in the foreground and placed themselves in the background.

The closest thing to gospel genre in the Old Testament is the narrative prophets (e.g., Jonah). But those books would only be cousins. While the Romans and the Jews used the term, it was not really applied to written literature until the writing of the New Testament (Mark 1:1). The Hebrew Testament had its narratives,[86] the Jewish literature had its parables and proverbs (far less anecdotal than our Gospels), and the Greco-Roman literature had its hero stories. But none of these are exactly like our Gospels. And we have the one gospel story told to the fourth power.[87] Said simply, the Gospels are inspired records, primarily narrative, and interpretations of the redemptive words and deeds of Jesus Christ and his kingdom for our salvation and service.

> The fact that the Gospels have held their ground throughout the church's history against incredible critique is nothing short of miraculous.

Each Gospel writer selected and sifted what he chose to say (Luke 1:1-4; John 20:30-31; 21:25). While the Gospels were written to specific audiences, the writers themselves put the words and deeds of Jesus in the foreground and placed themselves in the background.[88] They had already shaped the material (inspired as they were by the Holy Spirit), and they intended to save people by means of their Jesus stories. The subgenres are numerous and have many peculiarities. Here are several tips when studying from and preaching from the Gospel genre:

1. Put the accent on good news. Even John the Baptist found ways to speak truthfully to his audience and still give them *good* news (Luke 3:18).

2. In the encounters that Jesus had with people watch for the transformation of the listener. Where they are at the beginning of the conversation might be totally different from where they are at the conclusion of the conversation (John 4:1-42).

3. Audience analysis should be done carefully. There are layers here. You have crowds, disciples, the religion police, family, and

---

86. Much of what was said about Old Testament narrative genre could be applied to gospel literature and the book of Acts.
87. Scholars have written, taught, and debated for centuries how the similarities and the dissimilarities between the Gospels could be explained. Among them is a rough continuity, but there is also much discontinuity. It is my opinion that many of the differences have been way overexegeted and simply underline the different theological slants of the Gospel writers.
88. In fact, none of the Gospels are signed, unlike the Pauline epistles.

friends. All of these could frame up the original audience. But then there is the Gospel writer's audience (e.g., Theophilus). Then there is our preaching audience. If a preacher is not careful here he will always assume the role of Christ, which might not leave much left over for the congregation.

4. Jesus should be prominent. It is amazing how Jesus can be marginalized even when preaching from the Gospels. For instance, is the story in Matthew 14:22-33 about Peter having the courage to walk on water or about Jesus, whom the winds and waves obey?

5. Keep the story within that particular Gospel. This is only being fair. Don't preach a generic sermon about Jesus caring for people by healing them when dealing with a specific incident like the healing of the Centurion's slave (Matt 8:5-13; Luke 7:1-10). Those are parallel texts, but the writers tell the story very differently. The parable of the good shepherd and the lost sheep (Matt 18:12-14; Luke 15:3-7) sound at first hearing like an identical story. Not only are contexts completely different, the vast majority of the Greek words are not the same. There is a place for Scriptural harmonization, but don't over-do it.

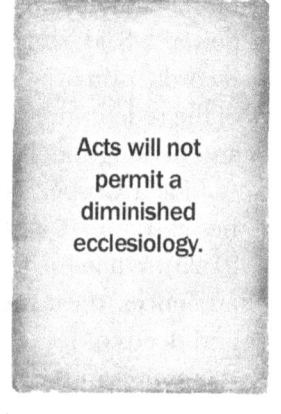

Acts will not permit a diminished ecclesiology.

6. Respect Gospel distinctives. Why does Matthew often have two witnesses of things that take place (Matt 8:28; 21:2)? Why does Mark have everything taking place at a rapid pace and cluster boat narratives (4:35–5:43) before bread narratives (6:14–8:21), which precedes blind people narratives (8:22-26; 10:46-52)? Why does Luke have a whole section devoted to the travel narrative and Perean ministry of Jesus (9:51–19:27)? And why does Luke invert things like the order of Jesus' temptations (4:1-13; cf. Matt 4:1-11) in the wilderness and the genealogy (3:23-37)? Why does John use double talk (John 4:13; 6:51; 9:41; 11:25-26)? Why does John place so many public claims and signs in the first half of the book ahead of the private time with the disciples in the latter part of the book?

7. Probe the subgenre to the best of your ability. One of the things that makes Gospel genre so involved (and exciting) is the volume of material to understand under each subgenre.
   a. Genealogy and birth narratives—connection to the Old Testament, proofs of messiahship, resumé of salvation, and Jesus as the new Israel.
   b. Parables—anecdotal comparisons that are shocking and subversive.
   c. Miracles—previews of coming attractions of salvation in its largest sense, i.e., the healing of all creation.
   d. Encounters—people left never the same.
   e. Discourses—preaching someone else's stuff.
   f. Passion and resurrection—third-day stories.
8. Change of event does not necessarily mean change of theme. A common theme can run through several paragraphs.

The fact that the Gospels have held their ground throughout the church's history[89] against incredible critique is nothing short of miraculous. At the end of the day, the Jesus story wins against all its enemies.

NT: Acts

Because Acts shares genre similarity to the Old Testament narratives and the Gospels, not as much attention will be given to it. But a few words are in order due to our religious heritage. As part of the American Restoration Movement (known in some circles as the Stone-Campbell Movement) Acts has been a centerpiece.[90]

Acts shares many similarities with the Gospels in terms of genre. Everything is looked upon as "acts." Speeches, miracles, dialogues, conversion accounts, imprisonments, and defenses are all acts. Remembering tips from narrative and Gospel genres will help. Here are some other tips:

1. Discern patternism carefully. There is in us, due to our fidelity to the Bible, an attitude that says, "If it was good enough for Paul and Silas, it's good enough for us." All well and good. But

---

89. Passion Plays began as early as the fourth century AD.
90. This would be true for other "restoration" type groups such as The Church of God (Anderson, IN.) and various branches of Pentecostalism.

keep in mind that recording the event does not necessarily mean approval of the event. Only go with "approved precedent" provided the context shows that the event has the approval of the author and that activity might be commanded elsewhere in the New Testament.

2. Observe the rhythm of narrative/discourse. Often the narrative events prepare the reader for the explanation of those events in the discourse. Don't allow those to get too far apart.

3. Trace the connection between geography/ethnicity and theology. Dr. Wayne Shaw said of Acts, "Geography is Luke's method, but theology is his purpose." When the gospel makes a leap geographically or ethnically it is usually underlining a new nuance of God's way in the world (i.e., theology).

4. Accent the church. There are many things involved in what might be termed kingdom missiology in the Gospels. But how did the people in Acts understand those kingdom concepts? They preached the gospel, baptized the converts, and planted the church. Acts will not permit a diminished ecclesiology.

NT: Epistles

It is stunning to realize that twenty-one of the twenty-seven books of the New Testament are epistles. In that sense the epistle genre is the dominant literary form of the New Testament.[91] If God could wrap the warmth of his love in his Son, then he could and did wrap the warmth of Christian doctrine in the form of a letter. This is probably the preacher's bread and butter. When preaching from the epistles[92] the application is low to the ground. We are reading what the inspired writer wrote to a church, and we are preaching to a church. So, the truth doesn't have to be abstracted much. I suppose that is why beginning preachers tend to turn to the epistles for their first sermons. Here are some tips to ponder regarding this genre:

> Pay attention to the rich benedictions and *doxologies*... they are devotionally powerful for the preacher and the congregation.

---

91. Jeffrey D. Arthurs, *Preaching with Variety: How to Re-create the Dynamics of Bible Genres* (Grand Rapids: Kregel, 2007) 152. In this genre section of the chapter I have not suggested many tools that specifically deal with the issue of genre and preaching, but this small paperback is a gem in that regard.
92. For our purposes here epistle and letter will be used as synonyms.

1. Follow the *flow* of the epistle. Narrative genre rests on plot. Epistle rests on argument. Progression really matters. Much harm can be done by using passages like Ephesians 5:22-33 as legalistic rules divorced from the doctrine that undergirds it (chapters 1–3).

2. Strive to accomplish something. Isn't that true of every sermon we preach? Yes. But epistle genre is "task theology"[93] and "performance literature."[94] It was intended to "do" something. Appeal to the will. Cheerlead for obedience.

3. Discern the *orality* element underneath the text. This might be true of most all genre of the Scriptures, but it is especially true of the epistles. The letter became a substitute for the personal presence of the writer (1 Cor 5:3; 2 John 12; 3 John 13). In this way it mirrors the concept of incarnation. But the epistles are primarily "polished sermons." Perhaps that is not a preacher's first thought when reading them. However it is most likely that the writer was pacing in his room (or jail cell) as he dictated the letter to a secretary (Rom 16:22). Strive to find the kerygmatic flavor to the letter. This should provide some preaching insights.

4. Find the *seams* of the epistle. Not only are these contextual markers and sermonic perimeters they also might function as liturgical breaks.

5. Pay attention to the *missionary* nature of the correspondence. The epistles have the flair of being written on the run (sometimes literally as the apostles were run out of town). The early church did their theology in the streets—not in the ivory tower. Let this missionary heartbeat come through when preaching from the epistles.

6. Balance *doctrine* and *duty*. There is a healthy interchange of those in most epistles. Often, for Paul, doctrine precedes duty but not exclusively so. They feed each other. Seth Wilson taught that the epistles were really doctrinal commentaries on the Gospels.

7. Consider the opening paragraph following the salutation as *window* to the rest of the letter. This is the contribution of William Doty.[95] Randolph Richards also adds that we should look for what

---

93. Fee and Stuart, *How to Read the Bible for All Its Worth*, 155.
94. Raymond Bailey, *Paul the Preacher* (Nashville: Broadman, 1991) 18.
95. William Doty, *Letters in Primitive Christianity* (Philadelphia: Fortress, 1973).

is absent in that paragraph as well.[96] This becomes very practical for the preacher. A book sermon could be preached from the opening paragraph in an expositional way.

8. Retain the *tone* of the epistle. These letters have tone as well as content. Strive to hear the music of the letter. Is the biblical writer angry, sad, joyful, or bland? This helps accomplish the text's *intent* discussed earlier in the chapter.

9. Pay attention to the rich *benedictions* and *doxologies*. Not only do these contain rich theology, but they are devotionally powerful for the preacher and the congregation. Examples might be: Romans 11:33-36; Ephesians 3:20-21; 1 Thessalonians 3:11-13; 5:23-24; 1 Timothy1:17; 6:15-16; Jude 24.

10. Consider *memorizing* and *quoting* an epistle as a sermon. What would it sound like? What would it say to the church?

11. Ponder what *rich themes* we would miss if we didn't have the epistles.[97] And, *explore* the new perspectives of Paul research being done.[98]

NT: Apocalyptic (Revelation)

We saved the best until last. Some might say we saved the hardest until last. Some might have wished that the chapter would have already concluded. So much has been written and preached from this genre to summarize the material is overwhelming. G.K. Chesterton is quoted as saying, "Though St. John saw many strange monsters in his vision, he saw no creature so wild as one of his own commentators." Fee and Stuart have it right when they say, "When turning to the book of Revelation . . . one feels as if he or she were entering a foreign country. Instead of narratives and letters containing plain statements of fact and imperatives, one comes to a book full of angels, trumpets, earthquakes, beasts, dragons, and bottomless pits."[99] Here are some tips to ponder when preaching from apocalyptic genre:

---

96. E. Randolph Richards, *First-Century Letter Writing: Secretaries, Composition, and Collection* (Downers Grove, IL: InterVarsity, 2004).
97. Themes like the universal lordship of Christ, righteousness of God and justification by faith, the church as the body of Christ, the mind of Christ, and moral excellence to name a few.
98. This emphasis is beyond the scope of this book. Writers such as N.T. Wright, E.P. Sanders, and James Dunn should be consulted for new ways of thinking about the law, righteousness, salvation, etc.
99. Fee and Stuart, *How to Read the Bible for All Its Worth*, 231.

1. Don't forget about the other *two genres* in the Book of Revelation. Besides apocalyptic genre, Revelation contains prophetic and epistolary genre. Harken back to preaching advice concerning those genres.

2. Discover the *setting* of the genre. The church is facing external persecution and internal cultural seduction. Both matter, but the accent might be on the latter.

3. Keep to the *code.* Apocalyptic genre is coded literature. The symbols have meaning that the original recipients had a reservoir of understanding to interpret.[100]

4. Follow the *retold plot.* Besides the two large sections of the book (chapters 1–12 and then chapters 12–22), there is something known as progression parallelism. This is where, instead of reading the book straight through chronologically, the reader is invited to read through the plan and judgments of God several times, starting with the first coming of Christ and going to the second coming of Christ.[101]

> Keep the accent on Christ more than the calendar. The key to the future lies in the past.

5. Discern the *deeper magic.* The conflict of this genre is not earthbound. Things with the Roman Empire and Roman culture were real enough. But the real battle is above us between Satan and God (see Revelation 12 for the best statement of this).

6. KISS (keep it simple stupid). Matt Proctor suggested giving people a simple outline of the Book of Revelation that they can easily follow. It might look like this:

   a. Jesus confronts the church (1–3).

   b. Jesus controls the universe (4–5).

   c. Jesus condemns the earth (6–11).

   d. Jesus conquers Satan (12–20).

---

100. Things such as beasts referring to empires and kingdoms; stars meaning angels; women meaning peoples or cities, horns meaning power, wings meaning mobility, and white robes meaning purity.
101. Clearly there are many God loving, Bible believing, and Jesus honoring people who understand the book differently than this structure. No one is sitting in judgment about their faith in Christ.

e. Jesus consummates his marriage (21–22).[102]

7. Keep the *accent* on Christ more than the calendar. The key to the future lies in the past. The decisive battle has already been fought by the lamb slain before the foundation of the earth.

8. Turn back to the *Old Testament*. The Book of Revelation uses the Old Testament more than any other New Testament book. It's not just Daniel and Ezekiel either. Heavy quotations, citations, and allusions come from Exodus, Isaiah, and Psalms.

9. Make it *square* with the rest of the New Testament. Dr. Marion Henderson (longtime teacher at Lincoln Christian University) used to suggest this, and it is wise advice. Whatever we make Revelation say, be sure it harmonizes with the truth found in the other twenty-six books of the New Testament.

Conclusion

The hard chair is just that, hard. Everything about it says, "Work." But the joy that comes to the preacher when good homework has been done is unspeakable. A great portion of this chapter concerned genre. Almost all the major genres in the Bible celebrate study. The narrative genre does (Ezra 7:10). The poetic genre does (Ps 119:97). The gospel genre does (Matt 13:52). The epistle genre does (2 Tim 2:15). No wonder that Rabbi said, "Rather would I forget my name than thy law, O Lord."

---

102. Matt Proctor, Class Notes from "Preaching from Revelation," in Advanced Biblical Communication Class, Spring 2011, 3.

CHAPTER 6

LETTING THE TEXT WIN IN A SENTENCE (JK)

By far the most difficult task for me in preparing the sermon is constructing the dominant thought I wish to preach. You may find it easy, but I never have. It is excruciating for me. Sometimes it feels like I am sitting in a dentist's chair. That one last wisdom tooth won't give, so the good doctor climbs up on my chest and tries to yank that stubborn tooth out of my mouth with a pair of vice-grips! I find the entire experience to be painful and often exhausting. Headaches and frustrations are often birthed as I try to find some kind of lucid sentence that will say what the text is saying in an engaging manner. I have made it a holy quest to collect the wisdom of what others have said about crafting this sermonic sentence. I have found this sacred search to be helpful to my own weekly struggle. The pain doesn't subside, but I do get a shot of needed encouragement when I meditate on these helpful statements. Read the following slowly and prayerfully.

J.H. Jowett, a fine late nineteenth and early twentieth century British preacher, said it well in his Lyman Beecher Lectures: "I have a conviction that no sermon is ready for preaching, not ready for writing out, until we can express its theme in a short, pregnant sentence as clear as a crystal. I find the getting of that sentence is the hardest, the most exacting, and the most fruitful labor in my study.... I do not think any sermon ought to be preached or even written, until that sentence has emerged, clear and lucid as a cloudless moon" (*The Preacher: His Life and Work*, 133). Almost everyone who has preached for any length of time knows this statement from Jowett and has accepted it as preaching gospel. I would simply offer a hearty "Amen" to Jowett's words. My students know that I believe what Jowett said is true. Sermons that are preached in class are often preached prematurely because the student has not done the hard and tedious work of building that sermonic sentence. Bryan Chappell has called this the "3 a.m. Test" (See *Christ-Centered Preaching*). The idea is that if we were awakened at 3:00 a.m. and asked, "What is your sermon about this Sunday morning?" we could respond with one crisp sentence. So many of us get bogged down in the mud of preaching when we have failed to find the necessary sermonic traction that one well-defined sentence can bring. Joe Webb said it as well as anyone has or can. "Homiletically there is some debate about the need for a bottom-line statement, a single sentence, as it were, that sums up everything in the sermon. When one is talking about preaching without notes, however, there is no debate" (*Preaching without Notes*, 46). I offer another fullhearted Amen!

Mark and I decided very early in our teaching and preaching ministries that we would work at not separating hermeneutics from homiletics. We realized, just like some of you, every time we preached and taught we were revealing to our listeners how to interpret Scripture. Believe it or not, when the preacher fashions the sermonic dominant thought, he is attempting to be hermeneutically sound and homiletically smart. Every year I suggest to new preachers and old ones that they re-read Warren and David Wiersbe's excellent work, *The Elements of Preaching*. This slender and yet muscular work can be read in less than an hour. Early in the book the Wiersbes declare that the intent of the sermon must be clear. "When the pilot does not know what port he is heading for, no wind is the right wind; and when the preacher does not know what he is trying to accomplish in his message, no service is a good service. . . . This sentence is to the sermon what the spine is to the skeleton, and the foundation to the house: it holds things together and helps to determine what the final product will become" (25-26). The preacher who wants to communicate clearly and effectively the truth of the biblical text will closely adhere to the wisdom of this basic preaching principle. The dominant thought is the map and compass of the sermon.

> ...if we were awakened at 3:00 a.m. and asked, "What is your sermon about this Sunday morning?" we could respond with one crisp sentence.

John Stott would remind us that every biblical text has a main theme, and every sermon has only one major message (*Between Two Worlds*, 224-225). "So then, in our sermon preparation, we must not try to bypass the discipline of waiting patiently for the dominant thought to disclose itself. We have to be ready to pray and think ourselves deep into the text, even under it, until we give up all pretensions of being its master or manipulator, and become instead its humble and obedient servant" (227). Well-seasoned messengers of God realize that the word they bring must be solitary in focus. Ian Pitt-Watson stated it strongly, "Every sermon should be ruthlessly unitary in its theme. This is the first and great commandment" (*A Primer for Preachers*, 65).

Sermons must be honed and crafted in a way that connects the text with the listener. Journalists understand the essential importance of connecting. Preachers could learn a great deal from those who write professionally. I suppose that is why Mark Galli and Craig Larson impacted me when I read their book, *Preaching That Connects,* in the 1990s. "A good sermon should drive home one thing, and if so, we can express it in one sentence. As good as that advice is, it's not good enough.... Each sermon needs an angle, a topic universal enough to concern most listeners and particular enough to spark curiosity.... Once we've determined this angle, every bit of sermon content should reinforce it" (48-49). The maximum effect that all of us desire to obtain in our preaching is greatly helped by sweating over this one sentence.

I find that if I can state in a sentence the essence of the text I've studied, as it might have been understood by its original audience, then I can move toward stating it in a contemporary one. I call this preliminary sentence the textual dominant thought (TDT). This is what Vines and Shaddix refer to as "the central idea of the text" (*Power in the Pulpit*, 130).

Several years ago I was preparing a sermon on Romans 15:23-33. The passage was a part of a larger series of twenty-five sermons that I was preaching from Romans. I more than realize that many preachers today work from the angle of a shorter series of sermons—three to five messages grouped together under some theme. I am finding, though, that many, including megachurch preachers, are returning to larger sermon series from single Bible books that they can carve up into smaller sections. Regardless of your opinion, what I am about to say is applicable to your situation. The study of the text, Romans 15:23-33, led me to write down this TDT: "Paul planned to take an offering to Jerusalem, visit the church in Rome, and then go on to Spain." That is what the text says and how it would have been understood by those Christians in Rome. The sermonic dominant thought (SDT), however, must be stated in a way that engages the listener and offers a large "So what?" The SDT is the application of the TDT stated in a contemporary manner. The theme or subject that Paul addresses is that of his own plans. So I took that theme and made it the focus of the message. I decided to preach that text indirectly and hold the sermon's dominant thought to the end. I opened the sermon by playing with the idea of how everyone makes plans, and I gave multiple examples. I then moved to explaining Paul's trip and joked about how other people's explanation of their travel plans can seem tediously boring. I then asked several questions based on the text about our own plans, talked about Paul's vocabulary, offered a number of illustrations, and finished with this sermonic sentence: "Everyone makes plans, but followers of Jesus surrender those plans to the One they worship." I trust the message connected.

The text must win over the sermon's sentence. Vines and Shaddix offer this challenge to every preacher: "Work hard at formulating your proposition. Work it, rework it, and then work it again until you have the best possible wording" (135). At this point, you may be asking several questions.

1. What should I call the sermonic sentence?

You can call it anything you want. It goes by a variety of names. Some refer to it as the proposition. Others like thinking of it as the theme, the subject, the statement, the message, the emergent truth, the controlling idea, the governing idea, or the thesis. All of these have strengths and weaknesses. My father usually referred to it as his sermon sentence. Craddock called it "the Eureka Point." Haddon Robinson uses the vocabulary of "the Homiletical Idea." Galli and Larson, as you may have noticed, like calling it "the angle." My old homiletics professor, John Webb, preferred using the language of "the central idea." Some even call it "the essence of the sermon in a sentence." Whatever you choose to call it, that sentence must crystallize what it is you are trying to say in the sermon. It is, according to John Stott, one of the key ways in which the sermon is different from a speech. Here we are saying in a fresh way what God has been saying in the text for centuries. The preacher must decide what portion of the subject he is going to bite off and chew. Most of us have a debt of gratitude for the help Haddon Robinson has given us. It probably is beneficial to hear his voice one more time. "A sermon has many ideas

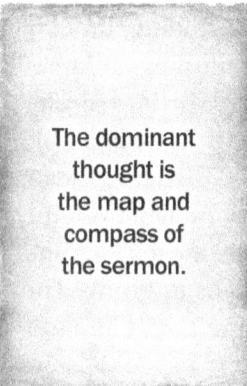

The dominant thought is the map and compass of the sermon.

to it, but all of them should grow out of the major idea of the sermon. That's not new with me. . . . When I talk about a big idea, I'm talking about an organizing factor. Take all the parts of a sermon and put them together into a whole, and that whole is the central idea—the big idea—in the sermon" (*The Art and Craft of Biblical Preaching*, 353). Regardless of what you want to call it, give that sentence a name so that you will be clear in your own thinking.

> The maximum effect that all of us desire to obtain in our preaching is greatly helped by sweating over this one sentence.

2. What can a dominant thought do?

The sermon's dominant thought can offer multiple directions to the message. This sentence can be a simple one that proves or disproves something from the text you are preaching. For example in Genesis 1 the preacher might say, "From the beginning God was Creator." Of course, the message would require lots and lots of "so what" for the listener to stay connected. Or perhaps a message is being preached from Genesis 3 and 4 where Satan, our arch-enemy, slithers his way into the narrative of the human race. The dominant thought of the sermon could be: "When I fail to trust God, all kinds of things get lost." The message would then unpack all the things that get lost when we trust the devil rather than God.

The SDT can be a truth from your passage that simply needs to be explained. It is probing something from the text that connects with the daily life of the listener. A book sermon from James could be shaped around this sentence: "The Christian life is an everyday proposition." The sermon would then be centered on the focusing question: "What does that mean?" An SDT can also exhort, persuade, or command something from the text, if the passage itself is shaped with imperatives. There are many of these kinds of preaching units in the Epistles. If the text to be preached celebrates something, then the SDT can be a sentence that captures the jubilant mood of the passage. An example or two might include: "God's grace knows no bounds" (Luke 15:1ff) or "Every Christian is a charismatic" (1 Cor 12:1-11).

The point of all this is to never forget that the SDT is the sermon in a nutshell. The listener should be able to say, "I know what the preacher is talking about, and I am following how he is trying to say it." Because this is so essential to the unity of the sermon and the listener's ability to track the message, I want to strongly underscore how vital the shaping of this sentence actually is. I offer below an example of linking the textual dominant thought with that of the sermonic dominant thought. This series of sermons was preached at the Jefferson Street Christian Church in Lincoln, Illinois. The church faced a lengthy period of time when spiritual conflict was surfacing in the life of this good congregation. The series was drawn from the book of Joshua.

Text: 1:1-18
Title: "Not All Is Quiet on the Western Front"
TDT: The Lord commanded Joshua, at the death of Moses, to be strong and courageous in his leadership.
STD: Spiritual battle is frightening, so spiritual preparation is vital.

Text: 2:1-24
Title: "A Battle for Keeps"
TDT: The Israelite spies entered Jericho at great risk.
SDT: Spiritual battle requires real faith from here to eternity.

Text: 3:1–5:15
Title: "Will the Real Braveheart Please Stand-Up"
TDT: The nation of Israel showed total commitment as they crossed the Jordan River to face their enemies.
SDT: Spiritual battle requires total commitment.

Text: 6:1-27
Title: "Let the Battle Begin"
TDT: The nation of Israel attacked Jericho at God's command and used God's tactics.
SDT: Spiritual battle requires that we fight God's enemies in God's ways even when those tactics seem senseless.

Text: 7:1-27
Title: "Sometimes There Is the Agony of Defeat"
TDT: Achan sinned and Israel suffered.
SDT: In spiritual warfare the way to fight private sin is with public confession.

Text: 8:1-35
Title: "Sometimes There Is the Thrill of Victory"
TDT: After being previously defeated, Israel attacked Ai and won the victory.

LETTING THE TEXT WIN IN A SENTENCE

SDT: Victory comes when I fight God's war with God's word.

Text: 9:1–10:28
Title: "Bloopers, Blunders, and Bombs"
TDT: Because the Israelites did not inquire of God, the Gibeonites were able to deceive the nation.
SDT: Like Joshua, we can make costly mistakes in spiritual warfare.

Text: 10:29–12:24
Title: "Onward, Christian Soldiers"
TDT: Israel conquered the southern and northern kings of Canaan.
SDT: Christian soldiers fight God's problems with God's promises.

Text: 13:11–21:45
Title: "Wanting Peace but Getting More"
TDT: In Canaan God gave Israel her inheritance of land.
SDT: God wants to give me more than peace.

Text: 22:1-24:33
Title: "This World Is Not My Home"
TDT: At the end of the war the eastern tribes returned home, Joshua gave a farewell address, and a covenant was renewed.
SDT: While we wait for the war to end, good soldiers trust the commander-in-chief.

These simple examples are intended to help you see the necessary movement from stating the textual dominant thought to that of preaching the sermonic dominant thought. I hope this proves helpful to you. Before we close this portion of our conversation, let me offer this strong word of encouragement. There are multiple reasons why the movement from the TDT to the SDT is so critical. Here are ten reasons worthy of reflection and application.

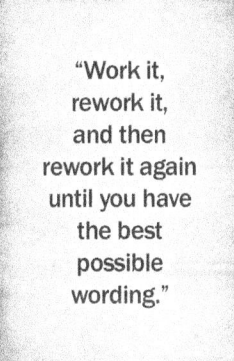

"Work it, rework it, and then rework it again until you have the best possible wording."

1. The SDT speaks to the single point of the sermon. It is a fundamental principle of good speaking of any kind.

2. The SDT gives the listeners a center upon which to focus their attention. It is a fundamental principle of good listening.

3. The SDT gives the mind and heart a definite focusing point.

4. The SDT identifies the single truth of the sermon and makes it memorable.

5. The SDT gives the listeners a solid foundation upon which to build their understanding of the passage and possibly their life.

6. The SDT gives clear direction as to where the sermon is headed.

7. The SDT serves as a point of reference for the entire congregation. They will apply it in multiple ways, but that one sentence can place the entire fellowship on the same page once a week.

8. The SDT gives the preacher his target. This sentence allows the sermon to be more like a rifle than a shotgun. The wise preacher knows that if the focus of the message is narrow, then he is more likely to hit the bull's eye.

9. The SDT can give profound clarity to the most difficult passage. The difficulty may be due to the listener's lack of understanding the text, the complexity of the thought or language of the text, or the fuzziness of historical and cultural conditions behind the text.

> The listener should be able to say, "I know what the preacher is talking about..."

I was preaching through Romans 1:18-32 recently. The passage is filled with talk of God's holy wrath toward people. It is a difficult but essential passage to preach if we are to reveal the whole will of God. So I decided that I would entitle the message, "What Happens When God Has Had Enough?" The title gives away the SDT. Because the text is so direct, I took the same path in the sermon. I attempted to describe God's holy hostility toward sin (1:18-20) and how vitally important it is to accept what He says about us. I then focused on the title's question and pushed the sermon along by offering answers from the passage: God has had enough (STD), therefore He allows us to search for false wisdom (1:21-22 and 28); He allows us to surrender to false worship (1:23 and 25); He allows us to seek out false intimacy (1:24 and 26-27). Then I asked, "Where is the Good News?" The sermon then moved to the last few descriptive words of God found in 1:25. I closed the message by describing the house that my oldest daughter and son-in-law purchased when they got married. Like most young couples they bought a house that needed some work. They did not realize, of course, how much work was going to be required of them. Somewhere in the process they discovered a major problem with the plumbing! Now my father-in-law, my daughter's grandfather, is an amazing man. Home and car repairs are his specialty, but he lives many hours and several states away. I got a phone call one evening from my daughter, and I could tell that she was frustrated and tired of the plumbing nightmare. She said, "Dad, I wish Grandpa were here. He can fix anything!" So it is with God!

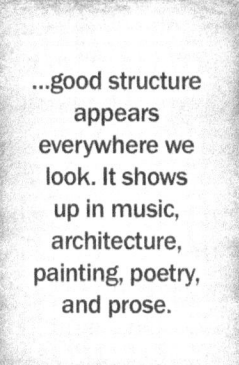

...good structure appears everywhere we look. It shows up in music, architecture, painting, poetry, and prose.

There is one other reason why the SDT is so essential.

10. The SDT allows everything else in the sermon to have a place to land. The SDT decides what gets into the sermon (introduction, illustrative material, structure, and conclusion) and what does not. If the SDT is weak the sermon will run over its banks like a river at flood stage. A strong SDT focuses and sharpens everything about the message. Therefore, all the sermonic material must be arranged to serve the SDT.

3. Can you identify the most important characteristics of any good SDT?

First, it is absolutely ***clear***. The SDT has a subject, verb, and object. It is a complete sentence. It typically is not stated as a question, seldom with one word, and never in a complex sentence filled with clauses and semicolons. It shines like an Illinois morning on a crisp autumn day. Second, the SDT is ***correct***. It says what the text is saying. It is accurate and truthful to the passage you are preaching from. It comes as a result of working hard to discover the meaning of your text then and now. Third, the SDT is ***concise***. It usually isn't any longer than fifteen or sixteen words. Of course, there are always exceptions to the rule. However, the SDT has one thing and one thing only to share. It is "lean and simple." Fourth, this sermonic sentence is ***contemporary***. I've been saying that all along the way. Yet I am still surprised by how many sermons I hear in which the central message of the passage is stated in the past tense or sounds like it was constructed for a lecture hall and not the worship service. The SDT builds a bridge between the ancient text and *your* contemporary setting. It is absolutely relevant and striking to *your* listeners. It customarily has plenty of "so what" in it. This is the place where you put the text into *your* own words. The preacher moves from asking "What does the text mean?" to "How am I going to say what this means in *my* setting?" The preacher can tailor any one of these four characteristics after they have tailored him. I recognize that what I am saying sounds "old school." I am well aware of the new homiletic and know that there are those who would argue that what I am advocating is antiquated. Maybe it is. I refuse to argue. I have devoted a large portion of my life to discerning how best to communicate the Gospel of Jesus Christ. I work hard at paying attention to what connects and what doesn't connect with my listeners. Apart from thorough study of the biblical text, this one application of shaping what the text says into a clear, correct, concise, and contemporary sermonic sentence makes all the difference in the world to the preacher and the listener.

A generation or two ago, Andrew Blackwood was one of the great preaching voices. He loved to remind preachers that good structure appears everywhere we look. It shows up in music, architecture, painting, poetry, and prose. The good voices of Donald Sunukjien and Eugene Lowry remind me of this truth. The sermon should not be left out of a culture that values clarity. Blackwood said that good structure is marked by unity, order, symmetry, and progress (movement). He seemed to take great delight in telling his students that the sermonic sentence influenced and affected all of the structure. He didn't care where the SDT or the "key sentence" occurred in the message. He said it could show up in the opening sentence, at the end of the introduction, somewhere in the middle of the sermon, or even at the end of the message (*The Preparation of Sermons,* 125-135). The wonderful news is that the preacher gets to decide where, when, and how the SDT will be revealed to the listener! Let the preacher proclaim a sentence that is tied intimately to the biblical text and yields itself in homage to that passage. The obvious challenge is to let the text win over that one vital sentence!

CHAPTER 7

LETTING THE TEXT WIN OVER THE SERMON'S SEQUENCE (MS)

Once the homiletical plotting is complete, once the text has won over the preacher, once the hard chair work is done, and once the dominant thought is extrapolated from the text, the preacher must make decisions as to the sequencing of the sermon. After all, as Jerry Vines reminds us, "Analysis is not the end of our work."[103] Andrew Schmutzer says, "But a 'loaded' laptop does not a preacher make."[104] Just performing word studies does not guarantee that lives will be put together. Gordon Fee states that sermons should be based on solid exegesis, but they are not intended to be a display of exegesis.[105]

The preacher must begin to shape all the study for the people. Obviously several predictable things impact the sequencing of the sermon. Congregation (audience), occasion, purpose, liturgy, and the calendar all play a part. Sometimes they even compete for the major role. The preacher must acknowledge their significance, and it is not unspiritual to do so. The Bible itself was not written in a vacuum. These matter, but they are not our concern here.

Memorable sermons often are a result of some device of sequencing that helps move the sermon along and lodge in the listener's ear.[106] It might be a controlling metaphor, it might be a refrain, it might be a type of homiletical structure such as alliteration, acrostic or verse-by-verse pesher style, it might be an imposed relational outline[107] or it might even be an all-encompassing illustration. However, the goal is not to achieve

---
103. Vines, *A Practical Guide to Sermon Preparation* (Chicago: Moody, 1985) 103.
104. Andrew J. Schmutzer, "Using Biblical Hebrew in Sermon Preparation," in *The Moody Handbook of Preaching*, ed. John Koessler (Chicago: Moody, 2008) 207.
105. Gordon D. Fee, *New Testament Exegesis: A Handbook for Students and Pastors* (Philadelphia: Westminster, 1983) 119. This advice must be taken with a grain of salt. Sometimes it is appropriate to take the congregation into the kitchen to see how the homiletical meal was prepared.
106. Tom Long [as quoted in Michael Duduit's *Handbook of Contemporary Preaching* (Nashville: Broadman, 1992) 168-169, defines a sermon form as "an organizational plan for deciding what kinds of things will be said and done in the sermon and in what sequence."
107. Andy Stanley and Lane Jones, *Communicating for a Change* (Sisters, OR: Multnomah, 2006) 46. Stanley has popularized the "ME-WE-GOD-YOU-ME" structure.

a cute outline. In fact a clever outline can be ruined by good exegesis.[108] "'What a marvelous outline!' is not the highest compliment a preacher can receive."[109] But the goal is to make the sermon portable and go home. Andy Stanley would remind us that the real goal of preaching is not information but transformation and application.[110]

When Aristotle Wins in the Sequencing

Without sounding too harsh, in Western Christian Civilization something besides the text has often won in sequencing the sermon. Put simply, it is Aristotle. The last of the most famous three philosophers of ancient Athens[111] did us much good in his classic, *The Rhetoric*. Where we would be without his famous logos, pathos, and ethos for good speech making? Frankly, for Western logic and linear thinking, that the Enlightenment took to a whole other level, it is hard to underestimate the contribution of Aristotle for organizing public discourse.

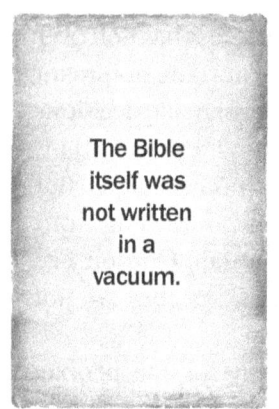

The Bible itself was not written in a vacuum.

While we are not opting for any Aristotelian idolatry, it might be good to give the philosopher his day in court before casting too many stones in his direction. Aristotle and others have established some good rules that have passed the test of time. We have found, in teaching many students to preach, it is much easier to get them to fly in formation once they have first learned the basic flight patterns. In other words, "You can break the rules once the rules have broken you."[112] Sequencing the sermon is a matter of arranging the elements of the subject (text) in such a way to achieve the object of the sermon. We are interested in establishing a logical pattern for the mind. This pattern does not have to slavishly follow Western forms. But to ignore good principles of organization is to do so to the preacher's peril.

Some preachers have railed against any Western form (e.g., the famous three points and a poem approach) that made preaching, at least in the English-speaking world, so predictable. They despise the *hard*

---

108. Warren Wiersbe and David Wiersbe, *The Elements of Preaching* (Wheaton, IL: Tyndale) 32.
109. Ibid., 31.
110. Andy Stanley and Lane Jones, *Change*, 96.
111. The others previous to Aristotle were Socrates and Plato. Aristotle was famous for many things such as being the tutor of Alexander the Great, identifying the syllogism, and defining words in terms of their extreme nuances.
112. Warren Wiersbe and David Wiersbe, *Elements*, 31.

sequencing that has come down to us. But what is offered in its place is often confusion. Following some preaching is an exercise in wandering in the wilderness. The Wiersbes remind us, "God is not the author of confusion, but some preachers are, and they do it in God's name."[113] So while we are not interested in Aristotle winning the day, we are willing to give him his due in helping us organize our thoughts for public discourse in the Western world. It is conceivable that some biblical texts might just carve up in rather predictable Aristotelian ways.

When the Text Wins in the Sequencing

Clearly the logic of the Bible is not always (maybe even rarely) the logic of the West. To allow the text to win in the sequencing[114] of the sermon we must "go where the text goes."[115] But how do we do that?

First, and foremost, preachers must make a commitment to be accurate to the text in the sermon's sequencing. This should go without saying since we have already established the importance of doing good homework on the passage in earlier chapters. But designing a sequencing of the sermon that is accurate to the text will not be automatic. It takes hard work to surrender thoughts about the text to the *lordship* of the text. We dare not preach falsehood. Our accuracy in handling the text is almost in direct proportion to our study of the text. We are attempting to let text have its own voice. We want the text to be the senior partner in the sermon. We want to present the text on its own terms.

Secondly, we will want to achieve a sequencing that respects the flow and movement of the text. Letting the text win demands not only that the substance of the sermon is extrapolated from the text, but it also demands that the flow and the movement of the sermon parallel that of the text. We can think of this process in terms of parallel lines:

1. _____ Bible (metanarrative)
2. _____ Text
3. _____ Sermon
4. _____ Stories, explanations, etc. (petite narrative)

---

113. Ibid., 29.
114. We are choosing to use the word "sequencing" because of its breadth. It matters little if the preacher refers to these aspects of the sermon as points, moves, structures, outlines, or developments.
115. Andrew J. Schmutzer, *The Moody Handbook*, 195.

The Bible contains the metanarrative of God's effort to get back what rightfully belongs to him.[116] It is a big and all-embracing story. Whatever we say in our sermon should always fit inside of that story. The text comes from the Bible and is therefore less than the total of the Bible. But the text is always bigger than the sermon simply because more sermons can be preached from one text. Then the supporting material inside of the sermon helps flesh out the sermon proper. But the largest thing to note is that all the lines are parallel. They all move in the same direction. When the sequencing of the sermon matches that of the text and when the smaller stories and explanations match the sermon, all of the effort will line up parallel to the large story of Scripture.

Some people talk about this idea of respecting the flow and movement of the text in terms of the coined words: hermoletics or homoneutics. Those coined terms combine the appropriateness of reading the text on its own terms (hermeneutics) and constructing the message in terms the congregation can follow (homiletics). Obviously this means that the preacher must have an awareness of context, content, and intent as discussed earlier.

> "The real goal of preaching is not information but transformation and application."
> –Andy Stanley

Thirdly, preachers will want to achieve a sequencing that teaches the content of the text. The importance of this was discussed in an earlier chapter. The preacher wants to teach the text as the sermon unfolds. The preacher wants to achieve an object in preaching, but the preacher also wants to teach a portion of Scripture so well that it leads to life transformation. The preacher desires that the people learn well a portion of divine revelation. The question is, "Which sequencing does that best?"

The answer to that question may depend on many things such as the listener,[117] the occasion, the season, the preacher's personality and gifts[118], etc. But putting those important considerations aside, it must

---

116. This idea is attributed to Gardner C. Taylor, famous retired African-American Preacher.
117. *Hard* structures might be resisted by certain audiences. There was a time in the Western world when audiences prized order, continuity, symmetry, and oratory. With some possible exceptions those days are over. In fact, in many circles in the postmodern world those things create suspicion. It would almost seem that disorder and tough sequencing are welcomed. In the current scene ambiguity seems to win the prize.
118. For instance some preachers are especially gifted in dealing with the *words* of the text. Others are good with the *stories* in the text. Some are especially keen in discerning *principles* from the text. Others like to work on *defending* the text.

be said that some methods of sequencing might be preferred to others because they accomplish more in terms congregational retention. Some sequencing allows the text to be taught better than other sequencing.

Preferable Sequencing

The most preferable sequencing of the sermon is the one that "goes where the text goes." This might be referred to as following the *progression* of the text. The preacher respects the text on its own terms. This sermonic approach is *direct*.[119] It is often didactic and usually deductive. It is straightforward. The preacher finds the "embedded" structures in the text and allows that structure to carry the exegetical freight to the people. When the congregation reads the text and hears the sermon, there is an immediate connection. The congregation's reaction is, "Oh, I see." It is what Dick Lucas called, "preaching the melody line of the text."[120] This method of sequencing helps the people to *learn* the text. A classic example of this kind of preaching would be John Stott's sermon, "The Greatest Invitation Ever Made," from Matthew 11:25-30.[121] The sermon *progresses* right down through the text from top to bottom.

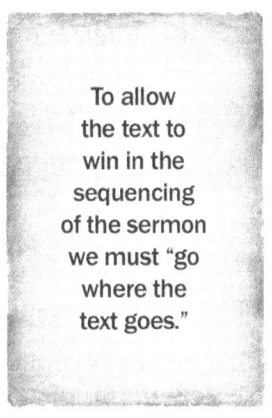

To allow the text to win in the sequencing of the sermon we must "go where the text goes."

The progressive sequencing approach works best on didactic texts and epistolary genre, but it is a solid method for many other passages and genre as well.[122] Walter Liefeld helps us by identifying twelve "compositional patterns" in a text.[123] The labels for these patterns will seem more accurate in some places than others, but naming these patterns will help the preacher to think through a text on its own terms and achieve a sequencing that is most like the text. They are listed here with the examples that Liefeld gives:

---

119. See J.K. Jones' wonderful essay, "Rediscovering the Direct Sermon," in *Preaching through Tears: Essays in Honor of Wayne E. Shaw*, eds. John D. Webb and Joseph C. Grana II (Lincoln, IL: Lincoln Christian College and Seminary Alumni Association, 2000) 53-62.
120. Dick Lucas, "Preaching the Melody Line of the Text," *Preaching Today*, Tape # 239.
121. John Stott, "The Greatest Invitation Ever Made," *Preaching Today*, Tape # 277.
122. It must be admitted that some passages will resist *hard* or direct structures. Certain types of narrative, poetic, prophetic, and apocalyptic genres will not always yield to this progression sequencing. This is why an awareness of genre can never be divorced from whatever sermonic approach is taken. Genre not only affects interpretation but also presentation.
123. Walter L. Liefeld, *New Testament Exposition: From Text to Sermon* (Grand Rapids: Zondervan, 1984) 60-72.

1. Comparison or contrast (Rom 5:12-19).
2. Repetition (Matt 5:3-11).
3. Continuity (Matt 13:24-52).
4. Climax (Matt 4 and Luke 4).
5. Cruciality (Matt 16:16).
6. Interchange (Mark 5:21-43).
7. Particularization (Matt 6:1-18).
8. Generalization (Matt 5:21-47).
9. Cause to Effect (Matt 21:33-46).
10. Substantiation (Matt 16:24-27).
11. Radiation (Matt 23).
12. Progression (John 20:3-9).

A preacher's comfort level with Liefeld's labels will vary, but his idea has merit. To let the text win, we must *progress* with it in the sermon. The preacher's goal here is to *find* the sermon that is in the text and expose it—not read a sequencing into the text that is not clearly evident within it. Preachers should want to deliver the goods not manufacture them.[124]

The sky might be the limit of how this sequencing that progresses with the text works. For instance if the text is the primary shaper of the sequencing of thought, then:

1. If the text is primarily *story*, then the sermon sequencing could assume a narrative format.
2. If the text is primarily *linear*, then the sermon sequencing could assume a logical explanation format.
3. If the text is primarily *illustrative*, then the sermon sequencing could assume an analogical or metaphoric format.
4. If the text is primarily *propositional*, then the sermon sequencing could assume an argumentation format.
5. If the text is primarily *encouragement*, then the sermon could assume an exhortative or hortatory format.

Six methods of sequencing will be mentioned here as *direct* meth-

---

[124]. John D. MacArthur Jr., *Rediscovering Expository Preaching: Balancing the Science and Art of Biblical Exposition* (Dallas: Word, 1992) 257.

ods of progressing with the text. First, there is the simple verse-by-verse (or phrase-by-phrase or section-by-section) "pesher" approach.[125] For preachers who feel that certain outlines and structures end up violating the text, this might be the best approach. At the very least it respects *how* the text does what it does. The temptation that must be resisted is the *commentary* sermon. Any forest theme can get lost in the structural trees. Preachers can be enamored by teaching little specifics, and context (literary, historical, and certainly theological) is lost. We are, after all, doing more than reporting on the details of the text. But we are also trying to leave no significant part of the text untouched.[126]

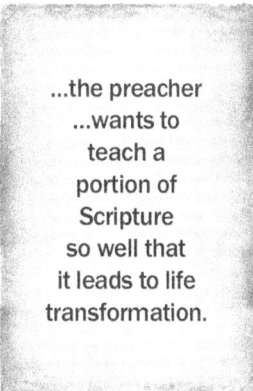

...the preacher ...wants to teach a portion of Scripture so well that it leads to life transformation.

When all other sequencing fails, return to the pesher method of our forefathers. The author remembers working hard on a sermon from John 3:1-15, Jesus' encounter with "Nick at Nite." After filling "file 13" with wasted approaches, a pesher style was chosen that ended up working well. The dialogue (subgenre) of the narrative/gospel text was respected, and the sermon took flight. The more harsh sequencing efforts ended in frustration. The text resisted the more imposed structures. Allowing the text to win by just naturally unfolding ended up being more satisfying.

Secondly, there is the carving up the text into pieces. This is typically called partitioning the text. The preacher's exegesis offers insight as to where the natural seams and joints in the passage are. The preacher might label these pieces, and those labels become the sequencing of the sermon. This kind of preaching has been the bread-and-butter style of many preachers in the West for generations. Its advantage is that the congregation learns the Scripture by paragraphs.

The author was preparing a sermon from 2 Corinthians 5:11-21. It is an involved passage that is theologically large. The contextual perimeters stretch from 2:14–7:1. Paul lays out his understanding of his ministry. Exegetical work exposed that the seams of the passage were verses 11-15 (although verse 15 could also go with verses 16-17), verses 16-17, and verses 18-21. The key concept was "reconciliation." The verse divisions

---

125. Pesher is from a Hebrew word that means, "interpretation." See Arthur G. Patzia and Anthony J. Petrotta, *Pocket Dictionary of Biblical Studies* (Downers Grove, IL: InterVarsity, 2002) 92.
126. Bryan Chappell, *Christ-Centered Preaching: Redeeming the Expository Sermon* (Grand Rapids:1994) 127-128.

became the sequencing slices of the text. The labels of those individual slices were generated by three basic metaphors that occurred during the study.[127] Using the theme of "Getting God and People Together," and asking the interrogative of "how," the sequencing went as follows: By Having a Clean Heart (11-15), By Having Magic Eyes (16-17),[128] and By Having an Articulate Tongue (18-21). The metaphors helped the sermon to be more memorable, but the slicing sequencing approach helped the people learn the passage by sections.

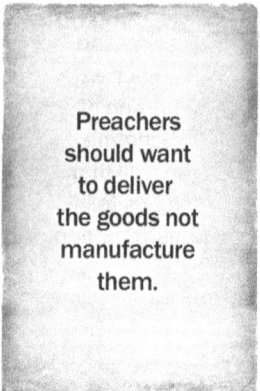

Preachers should want to deliver the goods not manufacture them.

Thirdly, there is the classification of the textual content. This approach was popularized by Charles Koller.[129] It may not differ significantly with the first two approaches and is often combined with them. In this method the preacher studies the passage and strives to label (or classify) the text. Key to this approach is the use of a plural key word.[130] The word is always a noun and sits as a directional header over the text. Maybe the text is about abuses, or answers, or aspirations, or consequences, or dangers, or essentials, or features, or methods, or qualities, or threats. The more specific the plural key noun, the better. Avoiding generic terms such as "things" or "thoughts" will advance the specificity of the sermon.

This approach might seem imposed and stiff at times, and there are snares to be avoided.[131] But when a preacher takes a portion of text and classifies it rightly there is a pleasing simplicity for the congregation.

---

127. Some will say that the metaphors were imposed since they are not specifically mentioned in the text. That would be an astute observation. But they seemed safely implied from the totality of the study. This just shows that the methods of sequencing often bleed together. Preaching is both science and art, and the two should not be separated. The Western world wants to categorize everything. Other cultures are not so hindered.
128. This label was adopted from Lewis Smedes from Fuller Theological Seminary in California.
129. Charles W. Koller, *Expository Preaching without Notes Plus Sermons Preached without Notes* (Grand Rapids: Baker, 1962).
130. Examples of such are listed on pages 53-54 of Koller's book.
131. Two dangers might be: 1) Imposing the wrong plural key noun on the text. The text might actually resist the classification. The preacher can usually sense this in the preparation. If progression of thought is difficult in the sequencing of the sermon, it probably is a clue that the preacher is forcing something. 2) Making all sermons sound the same. This is often referred to as cookie-cutter sermons. This method can be so attractive at first that preachers will begin to craft all of their sermons from this mold. So even if the content changes week to week, the congregation will sense they are hearing the same sermon. To the listener's ear, change of form may sound like change of content. Equally true is that similarity of form will flatten all the content and even "different" messages will ring with sameness because the sermonic method is the same.

Variations of this approach exist,[132] but the basic goal is to help the congregation understand the text in terms of one label.

A preacher in a former generation by the name of Don Sharp gave a good example of this kind of sequencing. He preached a sermon called "Operation Steadfast" from Acts 2:42. His classification plural key word was "ways." He combined the former partitioning of the text approach with classification with the following outline:

1. The Early Church Continued Steadfastly in the Apostles Doctrine
2. The Early Church Continued Steadfastly in Fellowship
3. The Early Church Continued Steadfastly in the Breaking of the Bread
4. The Early Church Continued Steadfastly in Prayer

Fourthly, there is the parallelism approach. In this direct sequencing the preacher takes note of obvious parallelism in the text. Bible poetry is filled with this method of communication. In fact, the second highest volume of genre in the Bible after narrative is poetry. Preachers need to become more familiar with this genre as it is all but lost from the homiletical arena today. Paying attention to the poetic parallelisms in the text creates insightful homiletical fodder for the sermon.

An example of the above might be Psalm 1. Two things are going on in the text, namely contrast and parallelism. The larger moves in the sermon could contrast the wise and the wicked. But the sub-moves would show the parallel ideas of each. The wise man does not walk in the counsel of the wicked, or stand in the way of sinners, or sit in the seat of mockers. On the other hand, the wicked man will blow away, not stand in the judgment, or be in the assembly of the righteous.[133]

> When a preacher takes a portion of text and classifies it rightly there is a pleasing simplicity for the congregation.

Sixthly, there is a chiastic approach. This is where the preacher notices some discernible rhetorical pattern in the text. It is often characterized

---

132. E.g., "stringing of pearls" (Jas 1:1-12) and "waves of the sea" (Eph 1:3-14). See MacArthur, *Rediscovering*, 225.
133. Textbooks on hermeneutics go into great detail about the type of parallelism evident in the text (e.g. additional, synthetic, antithetical, etc.). The value of this kind of identification for the sermon would be structural. Does the preacher have the same thing said three times or are there additional ideas each time (phrase) being stated?

as ABBA. The Bible contains chiasms much more complicated and involved than that. Sometimes they exist at a macro level.[134]

A simple example for illustrative purposes would be 2 Timothy 3:16. After admitting that Scripture finds its origin in God, Paul states that it has a fourfold practical purpose: teaching, rebuking, correcting, and training in righteousness. Notice the emphasis: positive, negative, negative, and positive. As the preacher nuances the differences of these terms in the explanation of the text, hermeneutical insight will give way to homiletical method. The preacher might desire to structure the sermon by reflecting this chiasm (ABBA), or the preacher might want to group the terms: positive and then negative.

Finally, there is the scenes approach to the text. A narrative passage can be handled *directly* or *indirectly*. It can give birth to either. But if a preacher wants the chronology of a biblical narrative to drive the sermon, then identifying the scenes in order can help the congregation follow the plot.

One of the most famous narratives in this regard is John 4. Jesus encounters a broken woman at a well in Samaria. Paying attention to the scenes will not only help the preacher process a large passage for the congregation but also fit with John's stated purpose (John 20:30-31). Scene one: the woman perceives Jesus to be a man. Scene two: she believes him to be a prophet. Scene three: she entertains the possibility that he might be the Messiah and, in turn, goes and starts a citywide revival. The people declare that he is the Savior of the world (John 4:42).

Once again it should be mentioned that certain biblical genres work better with these direct sequencing approaches. Some passages will resist this kind of more formal structuring. But preaching the text from top to bottom is a way to let the text win.

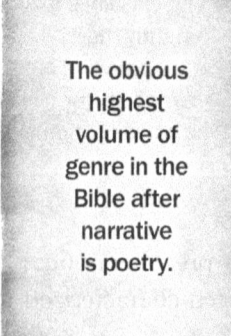
The obvious highest volume of genre in the Bible after narrative is poetry.

Alternative Sequencing

The text can still win even if it is not preached from top to bottom. There are other legitimate approaches in sequencing the sermon that still "go where the text goes." These might be termed alternative methods. They might seem to be more imposed, but they can still ring with biblical authority. In the former section we dealt with direct sequencing

---

134. See the whole book of Deuteronomy or the parable of the prodigal son.

or exposed models. In this section the accent will be on more indirect sequencing. The methods discussed here will be more inductive.[135] Four alternative methods will be mentioned.

First, a preacher could elect to *reverse* the text. This is simply where the preacher decides to preach the text upside down. Depending on the passage and depending on the genre this can work well. Not all Bible passages go from cause to effect. Some move in the opposite direction. Take Matthew 6:1-18 for instance. Verse one stands as the heading—don't wear your faith on your shirtsleeves just to be seen by people. Then Jesus illustrates that principle with citing three typical Jewish practices: Alms (2-4), Prayer (5-15), and Fasting (16-18). A preacher could use an alternative sequencing by simply reversing the text. This would allow the sermon to have an inductive flow and ending with the crescendo of verse one.

At a convention some years ago the author was assigned two passages from 1 John 3 and 4. The text was 3:14-18 and 4:20-21. The theme was, "Amazing Love Reconciles." Reversing the text seemed to help the sermon climax better. Even though an alternative sequence was chosen, there was still a discernible "harsh" outline. It was as follows:

1. The Responsibility of Reconciling Love (1 John 3:20-21).
2. The Risk of Reconciling Love (1 John 3:16-18).
3. The Reward of Reconciling Love (1 John 3:14-15).

Notice that whether a preferred or alternative sequencing is chosen, other homiletical devices can be chosen to advance the sermon. In the above example that device is alliteration.

Secondly, a preacher could elect to move in a dot-to-dot sequence. This too can create more of an inductive feel. Many things could dictate how the dot-to-dot approach will go (congregation, occasion, chosen passage or passages, etc.). Subalternatives in this regard might be sequencing the sermon with more of a spiral effect, or a circle effect, or a Socratic effect. Time and space do not allow the ability to illustrate each of these, but apocalyptic literature lends itself to spiral structures, African cultures can connect with circle structures, and Socrates' question and

---

135. Inductive models of preaching have certainly captured the attention of the homiletical world for almost five decades now. Fred Cradock, *As One without Authority* (Nashville: Abingdon, 1971) attributes H. Grady Davis, *Design for Preaching* (Philadelphia: Fortress, 1958) with getting this inductive method started. It gained steam with Eugene L. Lowry, *The Homiletical Plot: The Sermon as Narrative Art Form* (Atlanta: John Knox, 1975), and Ralph L. and Gregg Lewis, *Inductive Preaching: Helping People Listen* (Westchester, IL: Crossway, 1983). The most succinct statement of inductive preaching from the author's perspective is David Enyart, "Inductive Proclamation: The Question, the Quest, and the Discovery," in *Preaching through Tears*, 39-52.

answer method has worked for generations, and sometimes is a "when all else fails approach."

As ingrained as Charles Koller is in his classification method he gives evidence of this dot-to-dot approach. His sermon from Acts 2 would impress anyone from a Restoration Movement perspective. His three headings are:

1. This is That (2:16).
2. This is He (2:22).
3. This is How (2:38).

Thirdly, a preacher could elect to sequence the sermon narratively. This is different than what was mentioned earlier in the *direct* approach. This is also different from using narratives within the sermon (often referred to as illustrations or windows). What is meant here is designing the whole sermon in narrative format. Narrative becomes the method of sequencing the sermon.

This method was popularized by Eugene Lowry in his book, *The Homiletical Plot*. He took Fred Craddock's suggestion that the closest thing in the literary world to a sermon was a short story and ran with it. He said that good narrative has the following elements:

1. Upsetting the equilibrium
2. the discrepancy
3. Disclosing the clue to resolution
4. Experiencing the gospel
5. Anticipating the consequences

Or, said more simply by his students:

1. Oops
2. Ugh
3. Aha
4. Whee
5. Yeah[136]

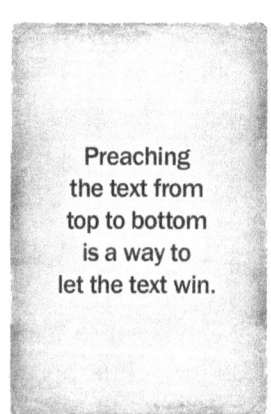

Preaching the text from top to bottom is a way to let the text win.

Some preachers will feel this is an alternative sequencing method that imposes too much on the passage. They will feel that it is more eisegesis

---

136. Lowry, *Homiletical Plot*, 25. See also Mike Graves and David J. Schlafer, eds. *What's the Shape of Narrative Preaching?* (St. Louis: Chalice, 2008).

than exegesis. Certainly that can be done. But as long as the preacher retains the hermeneutical integrity of the text this imposed structure can work well, especially in narrative sections of the Bible.

Finally, the preacher can elect to sequence the sermon analogically. This kind of preaching is very memorable. People remember analogies. Seth Wilson had a sermon entitled, "Married to Christ." He took the concept of marriage and applied it as an analogy to the Christian life. It makes 2 Corinthians 11:2 come to life.

Years ago the author was asked to preach on the theme of "Changed Heart." After tons of concordance work, the sermon got located in Psalm 51 under the theme, "The Drama of a Changed Heart." Since the audience was teens, analogy seemed the way to proceed. Barny Clark had just become the first artificial heart recipient. So three stages of heart surgery were traced and imposed on the text.

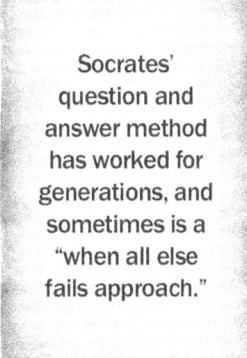

Socrates' question and answer method has worked for generations, and sometimes is a "when all else fails approach."

1. Diagnosis (1-5)
2. Surgery (6-12)
3. Recovery (13-19)

Another assignment was to preach on the theme, "How to Effectively Feed and Nurture Your People in Spiritual Growth through the Pulpit." The sermon was located in Nehemiah 8:1-10 and Ezra 7:10. The sequencing was analogical:

1. Create the Hunger
2. Set the Table
3. Prepare the Food
4. Serve the Meal
5. Clean up the Mess

Analogical preaching can be very engaging, but for the text to win, the preacher must ask if that which is imposed causes the text to be illumined or lost. The preacher wants the text to be remembered more than the analogy.

In the preferable sequencing models the text is more taught. In the alternative sequencing the text is more experienced. Both matter. The former matters so people learn the signposts of the faith. The latter matters, especially in postmodern times, so the faith does not seem so cold and stuffy.[137]

At the end of the day the preacher simply wants the text to get a fair hearing. The preacher wants the sermon to say what the text really says. One solid way to ensure that the sermon says what the text really says is to sequence the content of the sermon in such a way so the text can find a voice.

---

137. Other alternative sequencing methods might be refrain sequencing, "circle the wagons" sequencing (see Greg and Ralph Lewis' book, *Inductive Preaching: Helping People Listen.*), problem-solution sequencing, chronological or dimensional sequencing, or an interview sequencing. These are not as used as the others, but for variety can help the sermon achieve a good hearing.

CHAPTER 8
LETTING THE TEXT WIN OVER THE ILLUSTRATIONS (JK)

How do we find that "just right" and elusive sermon illustration? Most honest preachers admit the difficulty and acknowledge the necessity of the hunt. Stephen Brown says, "No matter how accurate our truth or how deep our message, if there are no illustrations, we have missed the very clear methodology of God: to make truth relevant with stories that illustrate that truth. . . . If you can't illustrate it, don't preach it. . . . By that I mean that if you cannot think of an illustration—a person, a story, a situation to which to apply the truth—then the truth is at best irrelevant or at worst simply not true. Truth that does not apply to real life is not worth preaching" ("Illustrating the Sermon" in *Handbook of Contemporary Preaching*, ed. Michael Duduit, 199-200). Illustrations do matter! If you preach very long, however, you will discover an agonizing truth. Sometimes our listeners seem to only remember our illustrations. They tend to forget what it was we were trying to say from the Bible. Ouch! With that in mind, several questions surface for the preacher.

First, does the illustration I want to use in the sermon help explain, illuminate, or apply the biblical text I am preaching? Second, does this illustration partner with or prostitute the text? Third, does the illustration that I am considering cultivate the drama and/or the day-to-day reality of the passage? Once again, we are faced with the unbreakable marriage between hermeneutics and homiletics. "Quite often illustrations have been restricted solely to the field of homiletics, but actually illustrations can fit securely in the field of hermeneutics when someone searches for meaning in a passage" (Harold T. Bryson, *Expository Preaching: The Art of Preaching through a Bible Book*, 194). Good preaching has always been colored by the use of image, metaphor, word pictures, and illustrative examples. Illustrations are the oxygen of a good sermon. They heighten interest, stimulate imagination, make content clearer, and offer tremendous help in applying the text, and making it memorable for the listener. Admittedly, those kinds of illustrations can be hard to catch. It is like trying to capture a mouse. Aggressive search seldom works. One must be patient. One must be careful in planning. I recall when my wife and I were living in an old parsonage in a very small central Illinois community. The church building and our home were located next door to acres and acres of corn and soybean fields. It was a perfect environment for communities of mice to thrive! Of course, when winter came on, the mice came in. We tried everything to catch them. We never met a mousetrap we didn't like. Most of the traps were marginally effective. We discovered, if we just waited and watched, the mice would come to us. Apparently their tiny lives were so boring that for them a good day of entertainment included running around our floors and furniture. One fateful and early morning, I was up early studying my Hebrew for seminary class. I sat there in my favorite chair with my Hebrew dictionary and Bible opened. I heard the pitter-patter of dainty mice feet running across the kitchen floor and into the living room. That mouse did what all mice seeking a thrill do. He ran up the arm of the couch, sprinted across the top, and stuck his sarcastic little tongue out at me! In that moment, like Moses lifting the stone tablets, I took up my Hebrew Bible and flung it at that pagan mouse. Charlton Heston would have applauded! I sent that rodent to mouse heaven! Patience paid off!

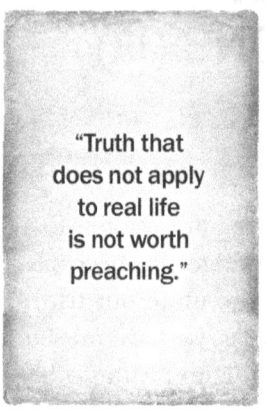

"Truth that does not apply to real life is not worth preaching."

Finding the just right illustration requires the same kind of perseverance. There is still clear and present danger, however. Sometimes the preacher finds a really fine illustration and can't wait to use it. In the next sermon he forcefully wedges that illustration into a place where it doesn't really fit. I've been guilty of doing that very thing! Remember, what is true of real estate is also true of preaching: location, location, location. Those same three rules are true of illustrations. Whatever you do with the illustrations that come your way, keep asking yourself, "Does this really fit into the text I'm preaching and the place I want to put it?"

Now we come to my major question: How do I let the text win over those elusive illustrations?

1. Don't hesitate to carry your text with you everywhere you go.

I take my sermon with me everywhere I go. I never quite know when

God will grace me with a story, an example, or an idea that illuminates my passage. W. E. Sangster's old analogy holds true here. He suggested years ago that the preacher function like a fishing trawler, nets out all the time, ready to catch anything that comes along, and separate the good from the bad later. These slippery illustrations can be found anywhere: the Bible, observation of everyday life, the newspaper, our own reading of books and magazines, listening to and conversing with people over a cup of coffee at Starbucks, web-sites, journal entries, personal experience, and many other places. Perhaps it would be wise to say it this way: Good illustrations tend to find us rather than us finding them.

People hand me things all the time. Some of them I can use and some of them I can't or wouldn't. Nevertheless, I never reject those well-intentioned givers. I find that, as I carry my sermon with me from place to place, I am much more receptive to thinking creatively and imaginatively about the text. Some time ago, as I was preparing to preach through the book of Acts, I was consumed by Dr. Luke's second volume. I was reading, thinking, writing, and praying about Acts all the time. I was working on my opening sermon in which I wanted to introduce the book to the congregation and found myself listening to public radio in my car. On this particular day Ray Oldenburg, professor of sociology at the University of West Florida, and author of *The Great Good Place,* was being interviewed. The book is a celebration of all the places where people hang out: cafés, coffee shops, bookstores, bars, hair salons, community centers, etc. He calls them "third places" or "great good places." Home is first and workplace is second. These "third places" are informal public gathering places where people seek community. Professor Oldenburg was describing the places that are at the heart of any healthy community. Never once did he mention a local congregation as a possible "great good place." He is in no way opposed to the local church, but neither does he seem drawn to her. I purchased the book, hoping to read something positive about the church. The only truly defining statement bemoaned the fact that the American Protestant church "far too often, sought to ensure the life of the church at the expense of the life of the community" (74). I decided in that moment that whatever I did in that

> Admittedly, those kinds of illustrations can be hard to catch. One must be patient.

series from Acts I wanted to paint a picture of the church as **the** great good place. In spite of birth pains, opposition, prejudice, disagreement, rejection, and personal threat, the church in Acts grew and thrived (Acts 6:7; 9:31; 12:24; 16:5; 19:20 and 28:31)! I am not sure if that idea would have struck me so hard if I had not had my sermon and pen in hand.

2. *Don't be afraid to talk about your text with the commentators and theologians—in front of your listeners.*

I know that some of you are thinking right now that my suggestion is suicidal. To suggest that the preacher look for an illustration in technical jargon sounds like a fatal flaw. I was preaching in Acts 12:25–13:53. My text was obviously large and full of detail. My study had led me to the conclusion that I had a legitimate preaching unit, and I did not want to shrink in size what I thought Luke was trying to convey. Here is a text filled with geographical markers, places, cities, miles, and travel talk. I wanted to help my listeners grasp the idea that inside my text Paul preaches a sermon that captures the story of the entire Bible (13:16-47). Paul knew the Scriptures, ached for the lost, and did something about it. All of this is shaped around geographical markers. Miles and miles of travel surround this sermon. I told the church folk I was convinced that Luke was saying something behind all this journey language. Maybe, I suggested, Luke was using some kind of literary device. "I'm not sure," I said. Then I quoted Barry Beitzel in *The Moody Atlas of Bible Lands*.

> ...what is true of real estate is also true of preaching: location, location, location. Those same three rules are true of illustrations.

The distances traveled by the apostle Paul are nothing short of staggering. In point of fact, the New Testament registers the equivalent of about 13,400 airline miles that the great apostle journeyed; and if one takes into account the circuitous (indirect) roads he necessarily had to employ at times, the total distance traveled would exceed that figure by a sizeable margin. Moreover, it appears that the New Testament does not document all of Paul's excursions. . . . Considering the means of transportation available in the Roman world, the average distance traveled in a day, the primitive paths, and rugged, sometimes mountainous terrain over which he had to venture, the sheer expenditure of the apostle's physical energy becomes unfathomable for us. Many of those miles carried Paul through unsafe and hostile environs largely controlled by bandits who eagerly awaited prey (2 Corinthians 11:26). Accordingly, Paul's commitment to the Lord entailed a spiritual vitality that was inextricably joined to a superlative level of physical stamina and fearless courage. (176-177)

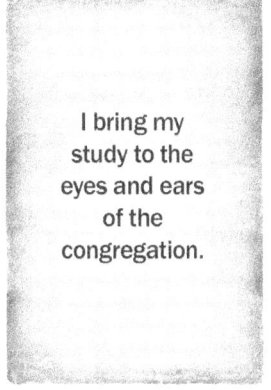

I bring my study to the eyes and ears of the congregation.

That's right! I took *The Moody Atlas of Bible Lands* with me into the preaching event. At that point, I could have said, "Paul traveled a lot like Jesus did." But by quoting Beitzel I not only get a well-crafted paragraph into the sermon, but I bring my study to the eyes and ears of the congregation. Someone might actually want to explore this great resource, *The Moody Atlas of Bible Lands!* I tied this illustration directly into my own personal example of walking in the early morning hours with Jesus. I said, "I get unction in my gumption when I do that!" Go back and look at my text. Does the illustration help the text to win?

3. Don't stop squeezing everything you can out of those good word studies.
Ron Allen says that word studies, more than any other part of our preparation, can walk straight from the study into the pulpit (*Contemporary Biblical Interpretation for Preaching*, 41). I greatly appreciate his insight.

> The difference between the meaning of a word in its historical context and in its contemporary usage can be so great that it is as hard to determine the meaning as it is to read license plate numbers in Denver while standing on Pike's Peak fifty miles away. . . . We try to position ourselves so that we hear a word with the same vitality and strength as it would have been heard by an ancient listener or reader. (41)

Often, these word studies paint pictures, provide analogies, offer illustrations and images on their own. A word of caution is offered: Please be careful not to convey your newfound knowledge in front of your listeners like a heavy machinery operator moving dirt. Sensitivity

LETTING THE TEXT WIN

and humility are always in order. We can become arrogant with our use of word studies. Nonetheless, these word study gems can be mined from the text and bless the listener in the process.

> Please be careful not to convey your newfound knowledge in front of your listeners like a heavy machinery operator moving dirt.

I was preaching from Acts 4:32–5:11, in which Luke offers two contrasted pictures of life in the early church in Jerusalem. On the one hand, believers are sharing everything they own with one another. On the other hand, Ananias and Sapphira pretend to do the same. When I was studying this text, I was drawn to the two-word phrase in 5:2, "kept back" (*nosphizomai*). Luke says that Ananias, with the full knowledge and consent of Sapphira, "kept back" part of the money they received for a piece of real estate they sold. Luke goes out of his way to make sure the reader knows that this couple could have done anything they wanted with the money. It was theirs to decide. But he wants us to know that something corrupting and demonic was going on. He informs us of this twice (5:2 and 5:3). My study revealed that the word has a long history of being viewed as misappropriating or stealing something. There is only one other occurrence of this word in the New Testament. In Titus 2:10 Paul urges Titus to teach Christian slaves not to "steal" from their masters so that the teaching about God the Savior would be attractive to others. I could have stopped there and driven home the point with an outside illustration. The search, however, was not over. I found in the LXX (the Greek translation of the Hebrew Bible) something absolutely illuminating. I used the following story as my illustration for what Luke was trying to convey.

> In Joshua 7:1 a man by the name of Achan "acted unfaithfully in regard to the devoted things." Israel had been warned by Joshua not to take anything from the city of Jericho because the entire city had been devoted to the Lord. The text says Achan "took" some of these devoted things. The result of his action was that a sin tsunami nearly destroyed Israel's military march through Canaan. Achan's sin hurt the entire nation. That one little word is used to describe the colossal dirty deed in the church at Jerusalem and in the camp of Israel!

I connected this word picture with something I witnessed at the

Atlanta airport as I was making my way home from Georgia to Illinois. I was tired and in need of a cup of coffee, so as I hustled to get in line at a Starbuck's. The man standing in front of me ordered his three dollar mocha and handed the waitress twenty dollars. She, in turn, counted up his change and handed twenty dollars back to him! Somewhere in her weary mind she had miscounted. He looked at all those one-dollar bills and almost walked away with a grin on his face. Instead, he paused, recounted the money, and returned to her what was not his in the first place. She thanked him and so did I. The word study not only provided me with an illustration, it connected me to another one!

4. Don't hesitate to craft your illustrative work from the themes and subthemes of the text.

Allow me to go back to the Acts 4:32–5:11 text. In that passage there is another repeated word phrase. The phrase "great fear" is inserted twice into the story (5:5 and 5:11). At first reading of the text those words don't seem very important. After further investigation and study, however, the fear theme seems to shape the passage. It begs a question: What scares you? There is nothing as exhilarating as being scared to death! All kinds of examples come to mind. When I was a child we played a game called "starlight-moonlight." The idea was to walk around the house or neighborhood singing the little ditty of "starlight-moonlight" and someone would jump out of the bushes and scare the living daylights out of us! I know, I know—that doesn't sound very scary. But, for six or seven little grade-school kids, it was frightening! What scares you? I'm a motorcycle rider. I know if I ever get to the place where I no longer respect that vehicle, I am a goner. What scares you? I will soon be married forty years. My wife is truly my soul mate. Though she is half my size, she scares me to death. I love Sue too much to intentionally hurt her. What scares you? The longer I looked at the text the more convinced I became that part of what Luke was trying to say was that anything— deceit, pride, lying, hypocrisy—could move into my life's center and cause me to love something or someone more than Jesus. What scares you? A simple theme or subtheme can unpack all kinds of illustrative ideas.

> A simple theme or subtheme can unpack all kinds of illustrative ideas.

5. Don't stop walking into the ancient background of the text.

By now, I hope you are noticing that illustrations often find their way into our preaching laps if we will just stay close to the text. The preacher doesn't have to create an elaborate system for finding and filing illustrations. Again, good study leads to good illustrations. For example, I've always been intrigued by the idea of "casting lots." I confess to you that I had not done a great deal of study until I faced it in a text that I was going to preach. Acts 1 describes, among other things, how the early church attempted to decide who was going to take the place of Judas as a witness to the resurrection of Jesus. Luke says they proposed two men: Joseph called Barsabbas and Matthias (1:23). The church prayed and then "they cast lots" (1:26). What does that mean? Is this timeless? Is it strictly bound by culture? Like any preacher who wants the text to win, I started digging into the ancient background and discovered that casting of the lots was a means of discerning God's will that goes deep into Israel's roots. I began to explore places in the Old Testament where the practice occurred. I saw that in Leviticus 16, on the Day of Atonement, Aaron cast lots for the two goats. One would be sacrificed and the other would become the "scapegoat." I noticed that in Numbers 26:55 God reminds Moses, "Be sure that the land is distributed by lot." Somehow, once Israel got into the Promised Land, everyone was to receive their piece of rightful real estate by casting lots. I also found this fascinating text, "The lot is cast into the lap, but its every decision is from the LORD" (Proverbs 16:33). My study led me to understand that typically names were written on pieces of stone or broken pottery, placed in a jar, and shaken until one of the names fell out. Those who cast the lots simply trusted that God's desire would be disclosed.

> The answer in the early church and the contemporary church is the same. "Everyone is responsible!"

The text I wanted to preach from in Acts 1:1-26 is clearly a prechurch passage. The Day of Pentecost had not yet arrived. There would come a time when casting of the lots would no longer be necessary. God would give each Jesus-follower the gift of the Holy Spirit. So, I wanted to know what this text had to say to the twenty-first-century church, especially the congregation where I preach. I kept asking that question over and over. I offered multiple answers drawn from the chapter: all of us are witnessing to Jesus' story; all of us are waiting for Jesus' return and need His power; all of us are watching for Jesus' answer to our prayers; and all of us are working at choosing Jesus' kind of leaders. I told the church that this reference to casting of the lots is the last such reference in the New Testament. A big question then surfaced for me: "Who is responsible?" There it was. An illustration found its way from the ancient background of casting lots right into my sermon. Not long before that I had ridden my motorcycle to the church building for one of our leadership team meetings. I parked it in the usual place. When I came out it had been relocated by some prankster. Of course, anyone could be suspect. There are plenty of folks in the church and the college who would take great delight in playing a practical joke on me. The first question out of my mouth was, "Who is responsible?"

> ...illustrations are not just something we add to the sermon like salt or seasoning in order to make it more palatable...

My wife made cookies not long ago at our house. It didn't take long for all of them to be eaten. When she wanted to have one with her coffee and found all of them gone, she asked, "Who is responsible?" Every year, in the life and witness of the Jefferson Street Christian Church, where I preached, the congregation would go through a six-month leadership selection process. There were discussions, interviews, suggestions, teachings, etc. The question inevitably surfaced, "Who is responsible?" The day of casting lots is over. The answer in the early church and the contemporary church is the same, "Everyone is responsible!"

6. *Don't stop listening to the "God-talk" of your text.*

I cannot emphasize this enough. It is absolutely key to finding those elusive illustrations. When the preacher continues to pray over and think on the "God-talk" of the passage, all kinds of sermonic windows begin to be opened. This kind of reflection gives the sermon size and "so what." I keep asking myself, "What is God saying about Himself in this text?" We can preach on that kind of stuff for a lifetime. It is a deep, clean, oceanic aquifer full of illustrative water. Not long ago I was preaching from one of the final paragraphs in Paul's letter to the Romans (15:23-33). I titled the sermon, "Surrendering Our Plan to the One We Worship." I opened the sermon by talking about how every one of us makes plans of some kind. I offered numerous examples. I suggested that Paul was no different.

He too made plans, and yet when I read his plans, something larger and weightier catches my attention. I asked several questions of Paul's plans and mine. I concluded that one of the great secrets of Paul's life was that he was both intentional and submissive. He intentionally made plans. There is nothing wrong with that, but he yielded those plans to God. When I was pondering that thought in my study, it stung me like a hornet. I thought about all those occasions when I had made my plans and simply wanted God to bless them. Instead of illustrating it negatively, however, I decided to put a more positive light on it. I called up occasions when my wife had done what Paul did in this text. I talked about the churches where we had served and how she so often was not allowed to use the full force of her spiritual giftedness because she was a woman. I described case after case when she set aside her plans. I wanted the listeners to think of Jesus. At the very end of the sermon I simply said, "Everyone makes plans, but followers of Jesus surrender those plans to the One they worship." So did He.

I pray that you will remember that illustrations are not just something we add to the sermon like salt or seasoning in order to make it more palatable for our listeners. Good preaching reminds us that illustrations are not simply supporting some point we are trying to make. Illustrations, like Jesus' parables, become the point!

...my thoughts than your thoughts.

"For as the rain and the snow come down from heaven, and return not thither but water the earth, making it bring forth and sprout, giving seed to the sower and bread to the eater,

...shall my word be that goes forth from my mouth; it shall not return to me empty, ...shall accomplish that which ...purpose, ...prosper in the thing for which ...it.

...shall go out in joy, ...led forth in peace; ...ins and the hills before ...ak forth into singing, ...trees of the field shall ...hands. ...thorn...

"Jesus loved to tell us about the Father,

about his will and purpose and

about his love and compassion for us.

He tried to tell us what the Father

and the kingdom were really like.

So again and again he tells us they are:

Like a man who . . . , like a mustard seed,

like yeast, like ten virgins, like a king.

When we listen to him,

we can always find a peg

on which to hang the truth he comes to share."

–Bob Benson, *See You at The House*, p. 104

CHAPTER 9

LETTING THE TEXT WIN OVER THE IMAGERY OF THE SERMON (MS)

Words matter. The person who said, "Sticks and stones may break my bones, but words can never hurt me," was an idiot. Words make the heart sing. Words send young soldiers off to war. Words can put a skip in your step. Words can send you to the slough of despond.[138]

The preacher wants the Word to win even in the words used in the sermon. When the Word has won over the preacher in his or her study of the text, has taken control of the dominant thought, guided the selection of the illustrations, and has given direction to the sequencing of the sermon, it is time for the preacher to do the actual wordsmithing of the sermon. The preacher begins to choose the words and imagery that will carry the message. This is like the creation account. God created the heavens and earth (Gen 1:1). But the form of this original creation was dark and formless (Gen 1:2). Then things started springing to life when words entered the picture. "And God said . . ." (Gen 1:3). Creation sprung up when the words got going. Preachers let the text win by careful, intentional, and thorough wordsmithing.

An Apologetic for the Words and Imagery

Remember that before there were words, there was the Word. Christ, the living Word, and God's historic Word were at work before the first words were spoken. His Word always precedes ours. His Word comes first. Our words follow. His words have genuine power. Our words at best only reflect his glory.

J. Wallace Hamilton said, "The transmission of ideas through words! No mystery is greater than that."[139] He goes on to say, "In the beginning was the Word . . . and since then a billion, million words have been spoken."[140]

---

138. This phrase is adapted from John Bunyan's classic, *Pilgrim's Progress*.
139. J. Wallace Hamilton, *Still the Trumpet Sounds* (Old Tappan, NJ: Fleming H Revell, 1970), 153.
140. Ibid, 155.

John Stott reminds us that we must speak what He has spoken.[141]

So the preacher begins to speak/write his or her words. When the preacher makes this move in sermon production, he or she is reminded of participating in a very ancient science. The first writing seems to have been done in pictures. Caves and early tablets show evidence that the pictures were maybe the earliest means of *written* communication. Perhaps preachers should take a cue from that. Speak in such a way that people *see* what is being said.

Brian Godawa has done profound work with this from an Evangelical posture.[142] He argues that theology and faith have overemphasized rationality and underplayed imagination. I get nervous when someone starts saying this, but he believes that the Bible is not a systematic theology of abstract propositions but a collection of narratives, poetry, images, and metaphors that convey God through both rationality and imagination. There is something to be said for a God who treasures aesthetic beauty. Preachers probably need to be less suspicious of artistic imagery in messages while engaging *both* sides of their brains.

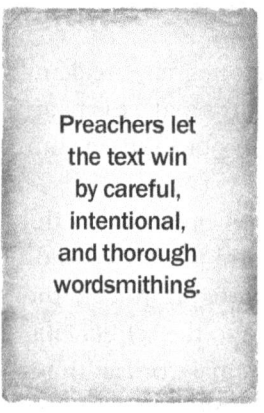

Preachers let the text win by careful, intentional, and thorough wordsmithing.

Clovis Chappell used to say that the chief characteristic of a good sermon is that it be interesting. My first reaction to that statement was not warm. No, the chief characteristic of a good sermon is that it be true. But Chappell would remind us that it doesn't matter how true it is. If it isn't interesting the parishioner won't hear it, and if the parishioner doesn't hear it, then it won't be true for them. Ouch. Even Albert Einstein was to have said that imagination was more important than knowledge. It is therefore a sin for a preacher to make the written Word sound like a dead letter.

When we speak of imagination and the use of metaphor in the wordsmithing of a sermon we do not mean to be taking flight into some fantasy island or mystic realm. Good imagination[143] helps us penetrate reality—not escape from it. Good wordsmithing in a sermon helps us see what is unseen (Heb 11:1; John 1:14; Col 1:15). James S. Stewart would remind us that even faith is a type of imagination.

It was a great privilege to have had as one of my teachers the famous

---

141. John R.W. Stott, *Between Two Worlds: The Art of Preaching in the Twentieth Century* (Grand Rapids: Eerdmans, 1982) 15.
142. Brian Godawa, *Word Pictures: Knowing God through Story and Imagination* (Downers Grove, IL: InterVarsity, 2009).
143. Such as is evident in *Pilgrim's Progress*, or *The Lord of the Rings*, or *The Chronicles of Narnia*.

voice of the "Back to the Bible" radio program for many years, Warren Wiersbe. He has written over one hundred books and has a personal library of over 10,000 volumes. In an essay[144] he reminds us that preaching is art as well as science. He states, "Hermeneutics and homiletics can give us the skeleton, but it takes imagination to put flesh on the bones. Homiletical scientists may be good at textual autopsies, but they cannot raise the dead."[145] It is one thing to be a craftsman; it is quite another thing to be an artist. Preachers should aim at being both.

Imagination, use of metaphor, and wordsmithing help in other ways in the message:

1. They help us *talk about* God. Without sounding overly philosophical, God is so infinitely beyond us that perhaps the only way we can speak of him is in metaphor. There is a sense here that all language is metaphor.

2. They help us know *what* the Bible is. It, like God, is infinitely various. It's all over the map and stirs the imagination.

3. They help us know *what* people are. Humankind is made in God's image. In part, this means that we can probably only speak of ourselves in metaphor.

4. They help achieve the *object* of the sermon. Preachers want the sermon to be portable and go home. To achieve that there must be a realization that the human mind is not just a debating chamber but also a picture gallery.[146] Vivid strokes help the picture to be more memorable.

5. They help in the *interpretation* and *appreciation* of the biblical text. More will said about this in the next section, but imagining oneself into the biblical narrative opens all kinds of possibilities for keen wordsmithing. This does not mean that imagination can run wild in what might be termed, "creative exegesis."[147] But becoming a thief or a leper cannot only help with one's sanctified imagination but also with the imagery one uses in the sermon.

---

144. Warren Wiersbe, "Imagination: The Preacher's Neglected Ally," in *The Art and Craft of Biblical Preaching: A Comprehensive Resource for Today's Communication*, ed. by Haddon Robinson and Craig B. Larson (Grand Rapids: Zondervan, 2005) 562-567. This essay first appeared in *Leadership*. The flight attendant story (562) is quite hilarious.
145. Ibid, 565.
146. This idea is attributed to Neil Dixon in his Gifford Lectures.
147. Said another way, "Off the wall."

6. They might help *anticipate* people's questions and possible objections. Sometimes just saying something in a different or fresh way opens up new ways of seeing something. This is reverse hermeneutics, where the rhetoric actually ends up driving the interpretive method.

7. They help *touch the hearts* and feelings of the congregation. The preacher aims at moving head, heart, and hands in a sermon. The volitional element is deeply affected by the rhetoric of the message. Therefore don't discount it.

I believe in multisensory preaching. I love it when all the senses are aroused through a fine message. Lights, sound, video clips, and maybe even fog machines (Lord, have mercy) can all be used to aid in the imagery of the sermon. However, a good wordsmith can do all of the above with his mouth. Don't forget that, the person who denigrates words and lectures on the impact of the visual dimension, used words to get the point across.[148] I remember that day in class when Warren Wiersbe told about seeing the Lone Ranger on television for the first time. He was greatly disappointed. The reason was that he had listened to the Lone Ranger on the radio for years previous to television. When he heard the words of the radio program his imagination went wild thinking of the masked man with his faithful friend Tonto. His imagination had outstripped the actual visual. There remains a significant difference between the real world of the human mind and imagination and the reel world of Hollywood.

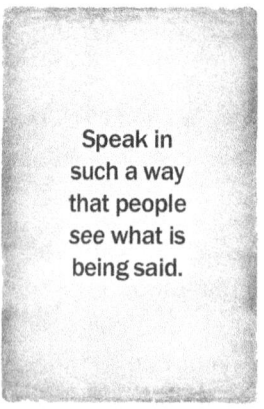

Speak in such a way that people see what is being said.

Picturing the Text

If the biblical text is to win in the sermon, then the actual *wording* or *imagery* of the sermon must driven by the text. Sometimes this is rather easy. The text itself might be filled with metaphor or images from which the preacher could draw. Examples might be some of the following:

- You are the salt of the earth (Matthew 5:13)
- You are the light of the world (Matthew 5:14)

---

148. See Os Guinness' chapter, "The Humiliation of the Word," in *Fit Bodies, Fat Minds: Why Evangelicals Don't Think and What to Do about It* (Grand Rapids: Bakere, 1994) 94-100.

- I am the light of the world (John 8:12)
- I am the vine (John 15:1)
- You are the branches (John 15:5)

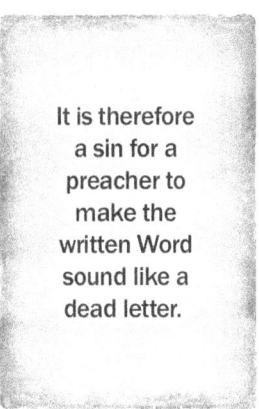

It is therefore a sin for a preacher to make the written Word sound like a dead letter.

A metaphor is composed of two unlike things. It is the bringing things like "A" and "non A" together. Thinking back through the above examples, people are not salt or light or branches. But Jesus is making that *direct* comparison. Jesus is not literally light (cf. 1 John 1:5), and he is certainly not a grapevine. But the images drive home (notice the metaphor) the points that Jesus can lead people to God, and that he is the new Israel that sustains God's people.

Whenever the preacher notices this in the text, some of the sermonic work is already done. Exposing those metaphors (images) as one preaches the sermons will cause people to say, figuratively if not literally, "Oh, I see." Even the language they use to describe such betrays how powerful metaphor is. We cannot *not* speak in metaphor—try as we may.[149] It is part of our linguistic DNA. And it seems to be transcultural. Even cultures without a written script use metaphors to communicate. Time and space constraints forbid us from making a list from Scripture,[150] but consider some of the following:

- The field is the world (Matt 13:38).
- This is my body (Mark 14:22).
- Go tell that fox (Luke 13:32).
- We are slaves of sin (Rom 6:16-17).
- Before meeting Christ we were foreigners and aliens (Eph 2:19).
- Christ is the foundation of the church (1 Cor 3:11).
- The apostles are the scum and refuse of the world (1 Cor 4:13).
- Christians are temples of the Holy Spirit (1 Cor 6:19-20).
- Christians are letters of recommendation (2 Cor 3:1-3).
- Christians were someone else's crown (1 Thess 2:19).
- The law was our tutor to bring us to Christ (Gal 3:24).

---

149. George Lakoff and Mark Johnson, *Metaphors We Live By* (Chicago: University of Chicago Press, 1980), is one of the most engaging and convincing books I have ever read on this subject. It clearly shows how metaphors are innate in us.
150. G.B. Caird, *The Language and Imagery of the Bible* (London: Gerald Duckworth and Co., 1980). This is an old work, but it is quite complete in its examples.

If any of the above are present in the preacher's text for an upcoming sermon the preacher will want to give pause in his preparation and sermon production. Those metaphors may well shape the dominant thought,[151] the sequence, and certainly the wordsmithing of the sermon. Don't rush over them as just "flowery speech." They help the preacher carry lots of the theological and sermonic freight.

But what happens when the imagery is not clearly evident in the text? Some metaphors are rather hidden in the text. Some are lost in the original languages and not evident in translations. Lee Eclov reminds us that sometimes the metaphor is a whole story or parable. Some metaphors are there by suggestion. Some are implicit.[152]

Warren Wiersbe gave solid sermonic advice when this happens.[153] He said when Scripture points to a concept drive it to a picture. When Scripture paints a picture drive it to a concept. Allow these to feed each other.

An example of this might be the famous armor of God passages in Ephesians 6:10-20. Certainly there is imagery embedded in the text. Fighting and battle imagery is used. Most obvious are the six articles of armor—connected by Paul himself to truth, righteousness, peace, faith, salvation, and the Word of God. More than one preacher has actually dressed in Roman garb when preaching on this text. But it might not be the best approach since the preacher is illustrating an illustration in the text.[154]

Knowing that people had heard this passage many times and thereby ran the risk of over familiarity, I decided, since the text was didactic and epistolary, that I would reverse it and go from concept to picture/story. My study of the text brought me to the conclusion that Paul was teaching four truths about spiritual warfare. Those were:

1. Find Your Strength Outside of Yourself
2. Know Who Your Real Enemy Is
3. Get Dressed
4. Pray Like Crazy

---

151. I would like to urge one caution here however. The dominant thought is a dangerous place for metaphor. Of all the sentences in the sermon this is the one sentence that should be pretty much straight prose. Filling the dominant thought with too much metaphor will cause people to go out scratching their heads. Be plain spoken here. Not many bells and whistles. And keep it succinct, too. See chapter six for JK's good pieces of advice about the D.T.
152. Lee Eclov, "What Makes a Sermon Deep? The Sources of Wisdom Preaching," in *The Art and Craft of Biblical Preaching*, 579.
153. Warren Wiersbe, Class Notes, "Imagery and Imagination in Preaching," Denver Seminary, summer, 1997.
154. Lee Eclov cautions about dissecting the metaphors (579). The preacher might actually destroy a beautiful picture being painted by the biblical writer. Leave the beauty in place.

Announcing those truths up front and working through them propositionally though concerned me for *interest* factors. I decided to tell four stories (remember that stories can function as metaphors). I did this even before reading the text. My goal was to lay the stories down over the text like an overhead transparency.[155] Once the people had the stories, they had the interpretation of the text. The sermon ended with reading the text and making a few *pesher*-style comments.

Another example might illustrate how to make use of the implicit metaphors within a text and within a portion of a sermon. In Mark 8:34–9:1 Jesus is calling us to embrace the cross as a lifestyle because God can always bring life out of death (this is the dominant thought). The text is composed of three things:

1. Imperatives (8:34)
2. Reasons for the imperatives (8:35-38)
3. Promise (9:1)

> It is one thing to be a craftsman; it is quite another thing to be an artist. Preachers should aim at being both.

Obviously a preacher would want to do the homework that would show that the first two imperatives in v. 34 are aorist tense, but the final imperative in v. 34 is present tense. That makes a difference in how this is preached in the *open enrollment* school of Jesus.[156]

In the next part of the text we see that Jesus is using *substantiation* as the rhetorical pattern in that verses 35-38 all start with the word, "for." So, we have *reasons* being stated. But probe deeper. The text reveals that Jesus uses rhetorical questions (he doesn't answer his questions in the text—nor do the disciples), economic terms (gain, forfeit, and exchange), and the language of paradox (saving ends up losing and losing ends up saving).

So how could we take advantage of the implied metaphors that are in the text for the structure and sequencing of that portion of the sermon? Maybe it would look like this. We need to embrace the cross as a lifestyle:

1. Because We Might Just Save Our Lives (8:35)

2. Because If We Don't We Might End Up Buying the Wrong Thing (8:36-37)

---

155. Does anyone know what that is anymore?
156. Notice that Jesus calls the crowds along with his disciples and then challenges all to follow by saying, "If anyone . . ."

3. Because We Don't Want to be Ashamed When Christ Returns (38–9:1)

Keep in mind that this is just one *move* within the sermon. But I was trying to take advantage of rhetorical devices (substantiation), economic terminology, and the figure of speech known as paradox to help frame up the sequencing of the sermon.

Exposing... metaphors will cause people to say... "Oh, I see."

The big idea here is that we want the text to win in every way—not just in the dominant thought, the contents, or the sequencing of the sermon. Some of the language available for wordsmithing the sermon and for painting the pictures for the mind are extrapolated from the text itself. They are most often in there if we look and reflect. In the same way that texts generate their own illustrations so texts generate their own imagery. Use it.

In a few other cases the imagery can be imposed from the outside—provided the preacher has done the homework so as not to violate the text. Let me illustrate from two wedding sermons. When our eldest son married I performed the ceremony. I took three imposed metaphors.

1. Marriage Is a Partnership (Gen 2:18-25)—it works best in the context of friendship.
2. Marriage Is a Duet (Song)—it never works as a trio.
3. Marriage Is a Play (Eph 5:22-33)—the success of the play depends on how well each person plays his or her part.

In another wedding sermon I took three Latin phrases and built the message around those:

1. Carpe Diem—Seize the Day.
2. Semper Fidelis—Always Faithful.
3. Ad Maiorem Dei Gloria—For the Greater Glory of God.

Each of the headings had attending Scriptures. My caution with this kind of approach however would be to make sure that the text really says what you are imposing. The value of such structures is how portable they are. They lodge in the memory and go home. It is to that emphasis that we now turn.

Smithing the Message

For the text to win, the imagery can often come straight from the text itself. But the preacher will always use words that are outside of the text as well. The preacher prays that through all of his or her words will come the Word. We are not fuzzy about which words in a sermon are God's and which ones are ours. The revelation from God is fixed—sixty-six books—no more and no less. But the document is living. So preachers use words to bring the Word.

"A man finds joy in giving an apt reply, and how good is a timely word" (Prov 15:23). "A word aptly spoken is like apples of gold in settings of silver" (Prov 25:11). "My message and my preaching were not with wise and persuasive words, but with a demonstration of the Spirit's power" (1 Cor 2:4). These *inspired* words should encourage us. But so can *inspiring* words. "For it is not enough to know what we ought to say; we must also say it as we ought; much help is thus afforded towards producing the right impression of a speech."[157]

We started this chapter by saying that words matter. But using the right words really matter. Mark Twain reminded us that the difference between the right word and the wrong word is the difference between lightning and a lightning bug. John Stott said that if a preacher preaches for forty years there is a strong likelihood that the preacher will use nine million words.[158] Case closed on using words well. Another man has estimated that if a preacher uses on average 3,750 words in a weekend message and preaches for forty years, that preacher would have written the equivalent of 500 books. And preachers wonder why they are brain dead following the weekend services.

> Some of the language available for wordsmithing... are extrapolated from the text itself.

The best advice I ever received about the words used in a sermon was from Dr. Haddon Robinson. He said, "Don't overestimate the people's vocabulary or underestimate their intelligence."[159] I preach in an educated community. The average education in my suburb is a Master of Arts degree. But I still have found this to be true. Even well educated folk like simplicity. A lively metaphor

---

157. Aristotle, *The Rhetoric*, 1435.
158. Stott, *Between Two Worlds*, 231.
159. Haddon W. Robinson, *Biblical Preaching: The Development and Delivery of Expository Messages* (Grand Rapids: Baker, 1980) 183.

will work almost every time.

Through the years I have collected philological advice in this regard from skillful homileticians (people like John Webb, John R.W. Stott, Haddon Robinson, Chuck Swindoll, Calvin Miller, and my dear co-author friend, JK Jones[160]). Here is the fruit of that list:

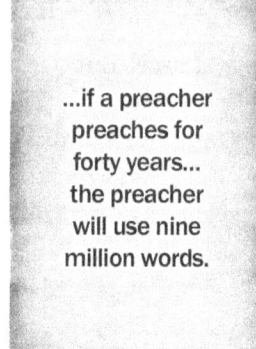

...if a preacher preaches for forty years... the preacher will use nine million words.

1. Master the grammar. There is most likely an English teacher in every church. We don't do ourselves proud when we use "I" and we actually should have used "me."

2. Speak clearly and simply. When students begin their study of Greek, they often read first from the writings of the apostle John. The reason is simple, his vocabulary was low to the ground. But that is not to say that his theology was not lofty. The goal would be to have the tongue of the people and the mind of a scholar.[161] Vance Havner said, "I want my message to go to the ordinary man. I'm feeding sheep, not ministering to a few intellectual giraffes."[162]

3. Employ vivid language (which is really the theme of this section of the chapter). Use language that appeals to their senses. Learn from the masters like Fred Craddock.

4. Use direct address. If you never say "You" they may not know that the sermon was truly for them.

5. Employ dialogue. Conversation in the Bible is interesting (Num 22:28-31). Why would we not expect it to be outside of the Bible?

6. Use specificity of details. The balance here is to trail off into word inflation and mere verbiage. But details help paint pictures in people's minds.

7. Use variety in sentences by especially paying attention to the use of strong verbs. Watch adjectival overload. Strive for forcefulness in the context of a conversational tone.

---

160. I would have to say that my co-author friend is a word whisperer. I have already booked him to preach my funeral because I know he will make everyone's heart sing. I continue to learn from him how to wordsmith. Reread his chapters and you will see what I mean.
161. Clyde Fant, *Preaching for Today* (New York: Harper and Row, 1975) 145-166. Fant describes what he calls "upper" garble and "lower" garble. Either way, it's still garble.
162. Vance Havner, *Pepper 'n' Salt* (Grand Rapids: Baker, 1983) 83.

8. Avoid trite statements—"like the plague." Otherwise, you will be "as dead as a doornail."

9. Work at building your vocabulary. Maybe one reason that Warren Wiersbe was such a fine wordsmith is because he was always working crossword puzzles. The larger the vocabulary the easier it is to select the exact word.

10. Remember that meaning is not just in dictionaries but also in people. Don't be surprised if you select a word to use and it really pushes someone's buttons.

When it comes to smithing the sermon there are some specific things we can do to enliven the message, make it jump from the pulpit into the pew, and travel out to the parking lot and go home. As preachers we can grow in our imagination and use of imagery in our preaching.

1. Expose yourself to imaginative sources. This includes the books you read, the people you hang with, and the experiences God's providence allows. I remember hearing Dr. Howard Hendricks say that by fifth grade our imagination (I believe he used the word creativity) has pretty much been shut down by average educators and their systems. However, Warren Wiersbe quoted Novelist W. Somerset Maugham, "Imagination grows by exercise and contrary to common belief is more powerful in the mature than in the young."[163] I guess we can still grow when we are old.

2. Draw or diagram your sermonic idea. What shape does it have? Is it most like a box? Circle? Diamond? Triangle? Preachers might be surprised what this will turn up. My advice would be to keep it simple. Some kind of detailed grid or matrix might makes sense to the creator of the sermon, but it might not do much to the listener.

3. Visualize the idea. If it is a biblical story, use your sanctified imagination to put yourself back in time. The caution here is to be conscious of the hermeneutical distance. Sometimes we err here because we haven't done our hard-chair homework about the historical background.

---

163. Warren Wiersbe, "Imagination: The Preacher's Neglected Ally," *The Art and Craft of Biblical Preaching*, 566.

4. Play another role in the event or story. Everyone wants to play the Good Samaritan in Luke 10:23-37. Why not see the story from the standpoint of the one left for dead? Or the thieves? Or the innkeeper?

5. Compare what you are talking about to a journey. This might help the whole message move more inductively, which usually accelerates the interest factor.

6. See the sermonic idea in relationships. Is it most like a family? Machine? Team? Business?

7. Question everything in the text. Have a childlike sense of wonder. Dumb questions can later be jettisoned, but asking *all* questions early in the naïve stage of your study might stir the imaginative juices.[164]

8. Take a crash course in learning styles. I love lecture. I am a linear thinker.[165] I enjoy taking notes and having the teacher be the conduit of information. But learners vary tremendously. Some learn best by story; not proposition. Some learn by doing. Others learn by discussion. Still others by reading and having times of solitude to process what was read. Some need community to learn, and others are learning hermits. Gather select people from your church around your desk as you write the message and imagine how they will best learn from this.

9. Pay attention to the creative cycle.[166] This rhythm might vary preacher to preacher, but Skinner lists the following steps for the creative cycle—informing, exploring, withdrawing, discovering, and verifying.

10. Experience cinema and theater. There are moral dangers here of course.[167] But perhaps God has left himself a witness in this

---

164. My experience with this has been that women are typically better at this than men. They seem to ask different questions of the text. Jill Briscoe would be a primary example.
165. Isn't that an incredible insight into the obvious given all the lists even in this chapter on imagination? Not very imaginary.
166. Craig Skinner, "Creativity in Preaching," in *Handbook of Contemporary Preaching*, ed. by Michael Duduit (Nashville: Broadmans, 1992), 565-568.
167. I'm not really just talking about immoral films that lack the kind of personal piety that God requires (Heb 12:14). I am also addressing the issue of how church people receive a phrase such as, "In the movie, Dumb and Dumber . . .", said enough the congregation will begin to wonder what the preacher does when he or she is out of the pulpit. Will they draw the wrong conclusion?

highly creative arena. For instance, is there a more powerfully moving piece on forgiveness than the recent musical film, "Les Miserables?"

11. Strive in your daily walk to connect the three worlds—natural, imaginative, and word worlds. An example might be John 12:24 where Jesus uses an analogy from agriculture. A seed can't produce anything unless it dies. Jesus is connecting the two worlds of natural life and spiritual life with the death of a seed.

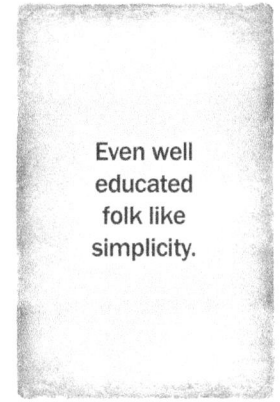

Even well educated folk like simplicity.

12. Spend time in the parables of Jesus. These are such incredible examples and literary masterpieces. They start out as true-to-life comparisons, then spring to fiction (where the grace element enters the story), and before they are over, they subvert and overthrow the structures of this world in favor of another.

13. Mix metaphors and play with language. This can actually be fun and funny. One fellow preacher that stimulates me in this regard is Paul Williams.[168] He spoke about the death of William Safire, speechwriter for Richard Nixon and Pulitzer Prize-winning columnist for the *New York Times*. Safire had some rules for writing: "Remember to never split an infinitive. Take the bull by the hand and avoid mixing metaphors. Proofread carefully to see if you words out. Avoid clichés like the plaque. And don't overuse exclamation points!!" Safire reminded his readers that language is always changing. Each generation thinks that their art of articulation is drifting into eternal night. "I can just hear William Shakespeare's mother's response upon reading *Hamlet* for the first time, 'To be or not to be?' Really, William, is that the best you can do?" Let me opt for 20/20 hearing. One person said, "If you can't take the heat, start firing back." Or how about, "She charged into my office and fired one rocket of criticism after another"?[169]

---

168. The selected quotes are from Paul's article, "And So It Goes," December 9, 2009 in *The Christian Standard*, a magazine that has been around since 1866.
169. A fun exercise is to consider Richard Lederer, *The Play of Words* (New York: Simon and Schuster, 1990). He has all kinds of things to do with metaphors starting on page 4. He categorizes them as light, food, nautical, car, and building-trade metaphors.

Concluding Cautions

Where there is much power there is the risk of a great explosion. Think of a nuclear power plant—much power and much danger. The same is true about imagery in a sermon. It can cause the soul to soar to heaven. It can also derail the train of sermonic content.

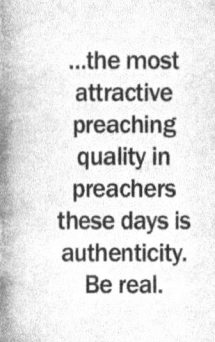
...the most attractive preaching quality in preachers these days is authenticity. Be real.

Some preachers, especially those with a strong right brain, will be drawn to this side of sermon preparation. That is good. There is plenty of room for you in the homiletical yard. But beware of using wordsmithing, imagination, and imagery as a substitute for solid biblical protein.

The temptation to be slick, flashy, manipulative, and showy is strong. It is fed by pride and the desire to be admired. Shun this. Perhaps the most attractive preaching quality in preachers these days is authenticity. Be real. When Jesus finished the Sermon on the Mount, the crowd didn't say, "Wow, he can turn a phrase."

CHAPTER 10
LETTING THE TEXT WIN IN THE BEGINNING AND THE END (JK)

Sometimes the difference between a good sermon and a great one is the time and effort the preacher takes with the little things. By little things I don't mean unimportant things: I'm speaking about introductions and conclusions. It would be wise to step back for a moment and recall how high the stakes truly are.

> Preaching is not some peripheral item in the program of the local church, but it lies at the very heart of what it is to be the people of God. It is clear from the NT that the primary means by which the church grew was through the preaching of the Gospel. . . . Preaching was not the giving of opinions or of reinterpreting old religious traditions in new and creative ways. Whatever the form of the proclamation the content was the Gospel of Jesus, and it was by this means alone that people were added to the church. (Graeme Goldsworthy, *Preaching the Whole Bible as Christian Scripture*, 32-33)

The sermon's starting and stopping place must be viewed through this bigger-than-life lens.

Two confessions are in order before we talk about beginning and ending the sermon. First, I confess there are some large assumptions that shape this chapter. I assume that by the time the preacher gets to the spot of wondering how to introduce or close the sermon much study and prayer have completely blanketed the entire preparation process. I am also assuming that the sermon's dominant thought, design, and aim are crystal clear. Second, I confess that there has been a monstrous debate over the subject of this chapter. Opinions abound. I do not mean to lessen any of those opinions or arrogantly pontificate my own. What I want to do is simply approach the subject with humility and honesty.

Introductions

Consider how important an introduction becomes in a relationship. I have met a lot of students' parents over the years. Not long ago, one of our graduating seniors wanted me to meet his family. He introduced them to me, and as we were talking, Dr. Tom Tanner, past Vice President of Academics of Lincoln Christian University and Seminary and dear friend, walked up and I introduced him to the student's mother and father. What I noticed was how delightful dialogue and small-talk took place because of a simple introduction. A good introduction makes conversation comfortable. What is true of relationships is true of sermons. Introductions are a part of everyday civility.

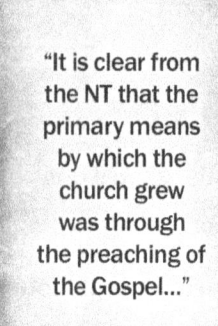
"It is clear from the NT that the primary means by which the church grew was through the preaching of the Gospel..."

Sometimes after I am finished preaching on Sunday morning, someone will come up to me and begin talking. If it is the last service of the morning, my wife or one of my children might come up and enter into the conversation. If I sense that the person I am talking with does not know my family, I will take the time to make the proper introductions. I have discovered that showing that same kind of sensitivity with my listeners makes all the difference in the world.

A good introduction is like a well-crafted opening sentence to a novel. Most of us are immediately hooked. Examples abound! For instance, consider Charles Dickens' marvelous skill in cracking open his stories. *David Copperfield* begins, "Whether I shall turn out to be the hero of my own life, or whether that station will be held by anybody else, these pages must show." When I hear those opening words I want to hear the rest of the story. Listen to Dickens' famous introduction to *A Tale of Two Cities*. "It was the best of times, it was the worst of times, it was the age of wisdom, it was the age of foolishness, it was the epoch of belief, it was the epoch of incredulity, it was the season of Light, it was the season of Darkness, it was the spring of hope, it was the winter of despair . . ." Even though the sentence is long and involved it still invites the reader to come inside. I want to know why those times were so strange.

Mark Twain's *Tom Sawyer* was my favorite book when I was a child. I must have read it a dozen or more times. I still like listening to that introductory monologue. "'Tom!' No answer. 'Tom!' No answer. 'What's gone with that boy, I wonder? You Tom!'" I want to know what Tom is up to! One of the reasons the Harry Potter series is so popular is that it is written so well. J.K. Rowling's opening to *Harry Potter and the Half-blood Prince* almost makes me want to become an addicted fan. "It was nearing midnight and the prime Minister was sitting alone in his office, reading a long memo that was slipping through his brain without leaving the slightest trace of meaning behind." I find myself laughing and I don't even know why. Even history becomes engaging when Stephen Ambrose lifts his pen and coins this line in *Undaunted Courage*: "From the west-facing window of the room in which Meriwether Lewis was born on August 18, 1774, one could look out at Rockfish Gap, in the Blue Ridge Mountains, an opening to the West that invited exploration." When I hear that beginning line I am already packing my gear, wanting to head out in search of a waterway to the Pacific. Nicolas Sparks creates this eagerness in his books as well as anyone. In *The Notebook* the story is introduced with these words, "Who am I? And how, I wonder, will this story end?" I'm immediately caught. I'm asking the same question.

Ernest Hemingway is considered one of the greatest English writers of the twentieth century. His life was a miserable wreck, but his writing was vigorous, tough, and alluring. Chew on some of these opening sentences in a few of Hemingway's short stories. "It was very strange in that house" (From *Landscape with Figures*). "Once upon a time there was a lion that lived in Africa with all the other lions" (*The Good Lion*). "The house was built of rose-colored plaster that had peeled and faded with the dampness and from its porch you could see the sea, very blue, at the end of the street" (*Nobody Ever Dies*). "That night we lay on the floor in the room and I listened to the silk-worms eating" (*Now I Lay Me*). "So he ate an orange, slowly spitting out the seeds" (*Banal Story*). "An old man with steel rimmed spectacles and very dusty clothes sat by the side of the road" (*Old Man at the Bridge*). There is something about Hemingway's style that drags me into the story, and I want to know more, experience more, and listen more. Magnetic sermon introductions are just like that.

> A good introduction is like a well-crafted opening sentence to a novel.

A good beginning to a sermon is like reliable transportation. It's like starting up a car and traveling toward a specific destination. My wife and I typically make a trip down to her folks in Arkansas each year. I find the start of the trip to be joy-filled. I begin thinking about the quiet reading time I am going to find. I start savoring the good meals my mother-in-law is going to make. I meditate on the beautiful scenery that will unfold before our eyes as we wind our way through the hills and valleys of Missouri and Arkansas. So much of the trip is lined by wandering creeks and meandering rivers. I consider the things I love about my wife's family, and I can hardly wait to get started. Few of us enjoy sitting in an automobile that doesn't go anywhere. No one likes to be packed, ready to go, and the engine won't start. Good sermon beginnings are like being brought on board a bus or train and going along for a scenic ride. Pleasurable starting places are like the beginning of a good motorcycle trip. The sound of that V-twin, the feel of the gas throttle, and the smell of a well-worn leather jacket nearly sends me into a state of heavenly ecstasy! There are multiple word pictures that can help explain the necessity of a helpful introduction. My favorite one, currently, is thinking about the introduction as the take-off of an airplane. When I hear the announcement, "Flight attendants prepare for take-off," when I feel the roar of those jet engines and the vibration of the plane, and when I sense the pilot is moving us skyward, I know the journey has begun! I admit that it still thrills me when this bigger-than-life-tub somehow gets into flight and I start seeing the earth fade from my sight!

I have spent a large portion of my life in and around airplanes. When I was in the military service my job included guarding rows of bombers and fighters. While in seminary and a student preacher, barely making ends meet, I was employed at a local airport to mow the grass and refuel, wash, and wax airplanes. As a preacher and teacher much of my time has been occupied traveling to and from locations that require flying. I don't know when it first dawned on me that a good metaphor for sermon introductions would be the take-off period of an airplane, but I truly believe that it is. One of the most dangerous periods of flight is when the airplane is taking off. Many crashes have occurred because something went wrong at the very beginning of the flight. After I get airborne I usually breathe a small sigh of relief. I think many sermon listeners are just like me. They tend to relax and become attentive if they believe

> Good sermon beginnings are like being brought on board a bus or train and going along for a scenic ride.

the preacher knows where he is going. Many preachers confess that the first three to five minutes of their message pushes the sermon into flight or causes it to tragically crash for their listeners. Introductions matter.

Like a pilot pouring over his checklist I find that raising a number of key questions is helpful. Experienced preachers tend to get sloppy, and inexperienced ones tend to stumble around a bit. These questions are intended to help us find that good starting place with the text we are preaching.

> ...a good metaphor for sermon introductions would be the take-off period of an airplane...

1. **Does the introduction stimulate a hunger or curiosity for the biblical text?**

   Quality introductions create a desire to want to hear the rest of the sermon. Smooth sermonic take-offs tend to accomplish at least five things. First, they make contact. The preacher brings the audience and the sermon together. There is a connection of some kind. Second, good introductions make sense. They reveal early on the basic concern of the message. Solid introductions offer a bit of the "so-what." Third, they offer the direction the sermon is going. The preacher might identify the problem being addressed in the sermon, the idea that is going to be enlarged, or the text that is going to be explained. Very few of us would get on a plane without first knowing its destination. Fourth, like good service on an airplane, somewhere in the first few minutes the need or want of the listener is addressed. The flight attendant might ask if the passenger would like something to drink or need a blanket or pillow. A wise preacher does something similar. He seeks to discover the need of the listener. The basic desire is to have the listener take the sermonic flight. If the sermon is going to be one in which the listener might be offended the preacher typically doesn't want to start out by revealing the sermon's dominant thought. Fifth, whatever happens in the beginning of the sermon, the preacher wants to introduce the primary biblical text. Typically, though not always, the preaching text is introduced, read, or alluded to in the first few minutes of the sermon's take-off.

2. **Does the introduction sufficiently open up the text's theme or subject?**

   There usually is that defining point when the listener has that "I-get-it moment." I have trained myself to watch for that when I am introducing my message. If I sense the congregation is bewildered or confused I will have to take a little more time to get the sermon airborne. Sometimes a little more runway is needed.

3. **Is my opening sentence crafted well and anchored in that passage?**

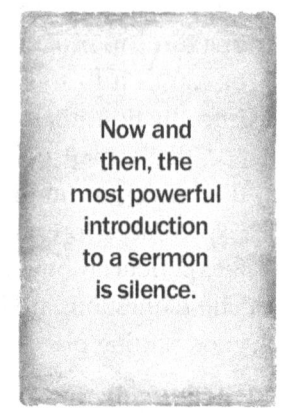

Now and then, the most powerful introduction to a sermon is silence.

I work hard at this. In the first few years of my preaching experience I did not devote a great deal of time to polishing and refining the starting line. As I have gotten older, I have noticed a significant shift in the attention I give to this sentence. My listeners have so many competing interests, and I like to get them ready for the flight quickly and firmly. When the airplane is about to depart, I find great comfort in knowing that a crew of very qualified people have thoroughly examined the aircraft to make sure it is flightworthy. I deeply appreciate the preacher who takes the same time and effort to be sure his opening sentence will fly.

4. **Does my introduction capture the head as well as the heart?**

I try all kinds of approaches in order to accomplish this. I might tell a personal story, draw on something from the newspaper, read a portion of a book that is written especially well, ask a question that I know the listeners are asking, raise an issue from the biblical text that creates tension, or admit to my own failure in light of the passage of Scripture. One of the remarkable things I have noticed about launching into the wild blue yonder is that there are no two take-offs just alike. Each is unique. Conditions change. Adjustment is required.

5. **Does my introduction talk about what people care about?**

I like getting at the "so what" all the way through the sermon, but I especially want to do that at the start. Good sermon take-offs are like jet fuel. They are loaded with plenty of "so what."

6. **Is there enough of the Divine in my introduction?**

Without sounding hypercritical or negative, I must confess that I hear a lot of sermon starts that have nothing to do with God, what He has done for us in Christ, or how and why He is at work through the ministry of the Holy Spirit. I'm sure I have preached some of those rather anemic messages. Even the shortest plane flight is filled with awe and wonder, when I consider all that takes place to get that airbus airborne. What the preacher desires for the listener to know and experience is filled with just as much awe, wonder, and even mystery. I can still hear Dr. Wayne Shaw's voice in a preaching class reminding all of us of the urgency of connecting the listener early in the sermon with God.

7. **Have I said too little, too much, or just enough in this introduction?**

I like asking this question. It reminds me to constantly monitor the length of the introduction. Every sermonic beginning is unique. So much depends upon the difficulty of the text I am preaching, what the congregation knows or doesn't know, and where the sermon fits into the larger framework of the worship service. My "take-off" imagery might conjure up memories of a flight where the pilot or attendant simply talked too much over the intercom.

8. **Should this introduction be presented with some "white space" (silence) before I begin to talk or should I begin speaking immediately?**

Now and then, the most powerful introduction to a sermon is silence. I cherish that old and wise preaching advice, "Start low and go slow. Hit fire and then retire!" If I were preaching from a biblical text that was shaped and colored by gray stillness I would try to duplicate that from the start. An example of this might be the story of Mary Magdalene, Mary the mother of James, and Salome in Gethsemane (Mark 16:1-8). They are visited by an angel, and the encounter leaves them speechless. They are trembling and bewildered as they stumble out of that tomb and sprint away in silence. When they finally speak, they do so with vigor and passion. I love the sound that breaks the silence. When flying a long distance, few of us enjoy nonstop talking. We value the well-placed sound of silence.

9. **If this is a direct sermon, have I sufficiently introduced the SDT?**

Never tire of asking yourself that question. I want the listener to grasp the problem I am tackling from the passage, why it is a problem, and what would happen if the problem were not resolved. If my airline ticket is stamped with Vienna as my destination, than I assume that is where my flight is going. Surprises are not warmly received. Take note.

> A good introduction is a lot like John the Baptist. As the sermon increases, the introduction decreases.

10. **If this is an indirect sermon, have I sufficiently created curiosity about the SDT?**

I want my listeners to go on this sermonic flight with me. I don't want to leave them behind. Always remember that good sermon introductions are marked by these vital characteristics: They are unified. They focus the listener's attention and do not confuse the thinking process. They offer clear transition into the heart of the sermon. They keep the listener buckled in. They are full of humility, that is, they do not offer more than they can deliver. A good introduction is a lot like John the Baptist. As the sermon increases, the introduction decreases. Above all, remember that good starting places are always served up in good taste. They avoid arrogance, scolding, mocking, fault-finding, sarcasm, and disrespectful speech. They suggest and entice.

Conclusions

The kind of sermons that allow the text to win not only begin well, they also end well. It is my biased opinion that conclusions are simpler than introductions. Of course, not everyone agrees with this premise. Just as bad things can happen when a sermon takes off, so those same bad things can happen when a sermon attempts to land. The airplane metaphor still fits. I have observed on more than one occasion passengers becoming quite edgy and anxious when the pilot hurriedly brings the plane down and bounces it several times on the runway. Just as there is a checklist for introductions, so I think there is for conclusions. Consider these questions.

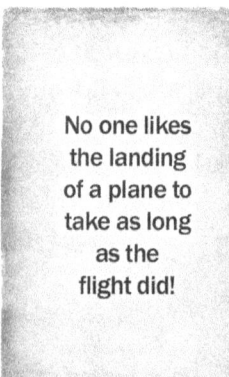

No one likes the landing of a plane to take as long as the flight did!

1. **Is my conclusion brief?**

Most of the old, classical thinking said that good conclusions do one of three things: They summarize, challenge, and/or appeal. There is a need for conciseness and narrowness of focus. I consistently caution my students not to make their conclusions too long. I absolutely agree with E.K. Bailey, "Brevity has immense power" (*Leadership*, Fall, 1997, 40). No one likes the landing of a plane to take as long as the flight did!

2. **Does my conclusion speak the listener's heart-language?**

I typically attempt to create a strong sense of connection with the listener before I close. I often use personal illustrations that my audience will recognize as their own story. In a series from Ecclesiastes I preached on the meaninglessness of wealth from 5:8–6:12. I wanted to end the message by challenging the congregation with the urgency of receiving and using their God-given wealth *now* to His glory. I drew on three memories. The first memory spoke of "The Millionaire," the TV show that captured my heart when I was a child. I told the church family about a shift in my thinking. My childhood memory is filled with dreams of receiving that million dollar check, but now that I am growing older I want to be the one who gives the million dollars away. The second memory was one of my brother and me in bed at night feeling hungry and knowing Mom had given us all she could for supper. We would lie in bed dreaming and talking of having McDonald's hamburgers, French fries, and Cokes underneath our pillows. I told the congregation that I used to think a lot about feeding myself, but now I think a great deal about feeding others. The final memory was one that involved my numerous trips overseas where I have encountered tremendous need. I conveyed my desire to meet needs rather than speak of my own needs. I concluded the message by saying, "Please don't fall prey to wishful thinking; ask God for wisdom-full thinking." Good conclusions compel people to make a decision. Again, I adhere to the counsel of E.K. Bailey. "The conclusion represents the highest emotional peak of the message, because I want to motivate people to do what they've just been informed about. I want to move them to action, not just agreement. People don't do what they *know* to do; they do what they're *motivated* to do. A conclusion must deal in the currency of passion" (40).

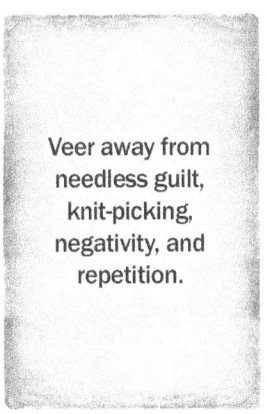

Veer away from needless guilt, knit-picking, negativity, and repetition.

3. **Am I absolutely clear about how I want the sermon to conclude?**

How I choose to bring a sermon to a conclusion depends solely upon the aim of the message. Sometimes there needs to be a clean break between the sermon and the invitation or the next part of worship. I personally believe that good conclusions bring the listeners to a personal application of some kind. What I want to avoid is announcing the end or falling victim to predictability. It would be wise to avoid these common crash-landings. Veer away from needless guilt, knit-picking, negativism, and repetition.

You can end with a question, a story, a quote, a summary, a hymn, a current event, or an invitation. Sometimes, however, the Spirit will intervene and conclude the message for us.

Veer away from needless guilt, knit-picking, negativity, and repetition.

A number of years ago I was preaching a funeral sermon at the gravesite of a young man who had taken his own life. The grieving father of the deceased was a friend of mine and an elder in the church. He and his family wept through most of the service. That young man had left a suicide note explaining his reasons for wanting to end his life. He spoke of how his wife had verbally abused him and how she had made their home life "hell on earth." Somewhere toward the end of my message the wife of the deceased came to that hurting dad and asked for forgiveness. She pleaded with the father to help her find peace. The conclusion I had planned was now out of my hands. The father began to explain to his daughter-in-law, in front of all of us, how in Jesus alone she could find the forgiveness and peace she was seeking. For the next five minutes he unfolded for her the Gospel story. Two weeks later she came to faith in Christ. Those of us who were at that cemetery that day will not forget how God visited us with His life-giving presence in that place of death. God's conclusion was certainly better than mine!

4. Does my conclusion match the focus of the text?

This may be the most important question for the preacher. A few examples may help. Nancy Ortberg once preached a sermon entitled "Modern Golden Calves" (*Preaching Today*, Tape 203). The entire sermon centered on her reflection of Exodus 32:1-6. She tackled the background to the text and then raised the question: "What takes the place of God in our lives?" She then listed a number of golden calves that all of us might be guilty of worshiping. Her conclusion beautifully and succinctly wraps up the message. "It is easy to read the story in Exodus 32 and think, 'Those silly Israelites.' But in Nehemiah and in Psalms and 1 Corinthians, the writers of Scripture come back to that story and remind those who follow Christ that we, too, are in danger of idolatry." When she concluded that sermon I immediately found myself doing a personal inventory of my own life. Good conclusions compel decisions.

Lon Allison, director of the Billy Graham Center at Wheaton College and professor of evangelism, preached a sermon he called "God the

Evangelist" (*Preaching Today*, Tape 210). The entire sermon focuses on God's role in reaching out to the lost. It remains one of my favorites. Lon explores the implications of Romans 1 and concludes that God is responsible for the results. He drives the sermon to an upbeat and celebrative ending. "Big D – Divine; little h – human encounter. That's evangelism. Big D – Divine; little h. Big D – Divine; little h. Big D – Divine; little h." At the end of the message I was saying those words with him!

One of my all-time favorite preachers is Tony Evans. He pastors the Oak Cliff Bible Fellowship in Dallas, Texas. I was listening to a sermon of his based on Matthew 7:24-27 not long ago (*Preaching Today*, "Building on the Right Foundation." Tape 264). Most of us know the text well. Jesus concluded his own teaching on the mount with a story of two builders, one wise and one foolish. Tony does a marvelous job of unpacking the meaning of that passage. As he draws the sermon to a close he tells the story of growing up in Baltimore, Maryland. He recalls the time his father purchased a balloon-boxing bag. Tony said, "You hit it, *boom*, and it hit the floor. *Bing*, it bounced back. *Boom, bing. Boom, bing.*" The base of the bag had a weight in it that was heavier than the rest of the bag. Here is how he finished the message. "I wish I could tell you that life had no difficulties awaiting you around the corner, but the Bible doesn't tell us that. God doesn't tell us that. Jesus doesn't tell us that. The Holy Spirit doesn't tell us that. So we shouldn't be telling you that. But what you can tell yourself, your family, or your flock is that when the storms of life go *bam*, you, because of the weight of Christ as your foundation, will come back *bing*. When all hell breaks loose, *wham, bam, bam, bam*, you're going to say *bing, bing, bing, bing*; because the man who built his house on a rock, after the hurricane was over, his house, life, family, and ministry still stood!" Now that's a superb conclusion that says what the text does!

A final word is in order. When all else fails and you don't know how to end the sermon, go back to the text. Let the text have one more chance to speak. The text you are preaching should be the control tower of your sermon. It offers you all the necessary data for a smooth take-off and a safe landing. Please don't circle the plane. Avoid staying on the taxiway too long. Get off the flightline. Never say, "Now, in conclusion." No one enjoys pulling up to the terminal and then being asked to sit there and wait. Few of us like promises that are not kept. Don't delay. Whatever you do, land the plane as well as you can! Your passengers may just fly with you again!

my thoughts higher than thoughts.

10 "For as the rain and the snow come down from heaven, and return not thither but water the earth, making it bring forth and sprout, giving seed to the sower and bread to the eater, shall my word be that goes forth from my mouth; it shall not return to me empty, it shall accomplish that which I purpose, and prosper in the thing for which I sent it.

"You shall go out in joy, and be led forth in peace; the mountains and the hills before you shall break forth into singing, and the trees of the field shall clap their hands. Instead of the thorn sh

CHAPTER 11
LETTING THE TEXT WIN IN THE WORSHIP SERVICE (MS)

Preaching is puny compared to worship. Clearly worship is the larger term. There is a danger of saying that all of life is worship.[170] Yet maybe that statement is not wide of the mark. Even after the etymologies of the biblical words for worship are traced and the words defined, one still feels rather helpless to get one's arms around such a huge theme. That is why this will be the shortest chapter. It's not because there isn't much to say, but that there is too much to say.[171] So this chapter will be just a small slice of how preaching interfaces with the worship service.

> ...this will be the shortest chapter. It's not because there isn't much to say, but that there is too much to say.

Throughout this book we have tried to be consistent in using the word "text" to refer to the biblical text from which the sermon is prepared and presented. In this chapter "text" will, for the most part, be viewed as synonymous with "preaching." To some extent this is a real stretch. We have already established that the revelation from God is objective. The words of the sermon are not equated with God's Word. However when we discuss the interface of the preaching of the Word in a corporate worship service we are thinking of the full meal deal (the reading of the passage and its exposure and application to the people).[172]

Preaching is for the church. Not all would agree. Some have opted for distinguishing teaching and preaching. For some the distinction

---

170. If everything is worship, then maybe nothing is worship and we have emptied the term. When the Bible talks about God's people worshiping, it no doubt has *something* in mind. However, the words for worship refer both to bowing down in reverence and to service. That encompasses lots of life. This may be why Donald Carson says, "There was no need to exhort human beings in worship (speaking of creation); their entire existence revolved around the God who had made them" [Donald Carson, "Worship under the Word," in *Worship by the Book*, ed. by Donald Carson (Grand Rapids: Zondervan, 2002) 34].
171. In addition I feel incapable of tackling such a huge subject.
172. Keep in mind that in the Reformation Movement (and not in a New-Orthodox way) preaching of the Word of God *was* the Word of God. There is a sense in which that is true.

is sharp. Preaching is for the unchurched and teaching is for the churched.[173] I am old enough to remember when the Sunday Evening Service (yes there was such a thing) was called the "evangelistic hour." This morphed into the seeker sensitive (driven?) services of the 1970s–1990s (primarily in the West) where the worship service and the sermon were all designed to do evangelism "at church."[174]

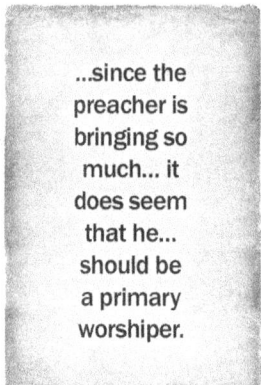

...since the preacher is bringing so much... it does seem that he... should be a primary worshiper.

Without getting lost in semantics I would like to circle back and say again, "preaching is for the church." If preaching is a negative term (hopefully not after reading this book), then so be it. Substitute another term.[175] But at some point in the gathering of Christians to worship God, a substantial amount of time will be given to the preaching of the written Word of God in the service. This chapter is concerned with that.

The Preacher as Worshiper and Member of the Worship Team

I get nervous when I hear statements like, "Preaching is the most important part of the worship service." Where is the proof text for that? Of course I get equally nervous when I hear the same statement made about communion, offering (does anyone say that about giving?), prayers, or singing.[176] Preaching might be the longest part of the typical worship service, but the most important?

Having said that, since the preacher is bringing so much to the worship service, it does seem that he or she should be a primary worshiper. Stephen Olford taught that when a preacher finishes the sermon, he or she should get on his or her knees and prayerfully relate the message to

---

173. C.H. Dodd, *The Apostolic Preaching and Its Development* (Grand Rapids: Baker, 1980), was a strong advocate of this position. "*Kerugma*" took place for unbelievers while "*didachē*" took place for believers. For people within the Restoration Movement heritage, it should be noted that one hundred years before Dodd, Alexander Campbell thought much the same thing. But the distinction is hard to maintain linguistically. While there must be some nuance of difference between the terms—they do, after all, occur side by side in the same verses (Matthew 4:23; 9:35)—they greatly overlap. All good preaching has some teaching content in it. It is not all announcement and inspiration. Similarly all good teaching has some good exhortation in it and is not just a conduit for information. Compare footnote 11 on page 28.
174. I am mentioning these things as historical markers. I am not criticizing them. Many people owe their salvation to such an approach.
175. Although "share" doesn't do much for me.
176. Singing might be most interesting of all in our day. Worship has become a synonym for singing. I am not sure how that happened.

God as a devotional exercise to prepare the heart to worship.[177] James S. Stewart taught that more than anything the preacher should be a person of prayer.[178] If the preacher has been praying without ceasing (1 Thess 5:17) and has been listening to the Word all week, the people will want to know what he or she has been hearing from God.

In this sense the preacher is a primary worshiper. But he also participates with his or her fellow worship prompters. It's proper for the preacher to be part of the worship team. It may not be possible in large churches for preachers (they also function as senior leaders in the church and have extremely busy schedules) to attend the worship team meetings or rehearsals, but his or her role in such is significant. The only way a coordinated effort of worship can be experienced is if the preacher is a fellow prompter along with those who serve in music, meditations, prayer, etc. Most worship team members will welcome the preacher's input concerning the total service and particularly his input regarding the message for the service. It is also advantageous for the preacher to learn whatever the worship team members are thinking about the service.

Preaching as Worship

Again, we must be careful here with our wording. If everything is worship then maybe nothing is worship (cf. footnote 172). The word, "worship," has to do with bowing down to God in reverence. Preaching, strictly speaking, is not that. However, there is a sense in which what the preacher offers in the service is an *expression* of his worship to God. All Christians are commanded to contribute something to the service. We may not bring an animal for sacrifice anymore due to the

> Robert Smith speaks of the preacher acting as an exegetical escort for the doctrinal dance so that the worshiper can be transformed.

new covenant, but we are to, at the very least, bring a sacrifice of praise (Heb 13:15) and bring something for the body (1 Cor 14:26). There is also a sense in which preaching is a congregational function.[179]

Just as the music team brings their best song, and those who prepare

---

177. Stephen F. Olford and David L. Olford, *Anointed Expository Preaching* (Nashville: Broadman and Holman, 1998) 312-322.
178. This is in a handwritten letter from Stewart that I have in my files. It was not written to me, but I was able to obtain a copy of it from a preacher in Joplin, Missouri.
179. I personally like to come from the congregation to the stage to preach. I am not keen on coming out from behind stage. I have no criticism here for those who prefer that practice. I just enjoy the *theological feeling* of coming out of the congregation to preach. I have been worshiping with them, and now they (sort of) come with me to preach.

communion bring their cleanest trays, and those who adjust buttons at the sound board in the back of the room strive for perfect sound, and those who work up meditations do so with prayerful consideration of occasion, setting, and audience, and those who clean the building do so with the attitude of Brother Andrew,[180] so the preacher brings his best for the teaching of the church. It is part of his or her giftedness and calling. Robert Smith speaks of the preacher acting as an exegetical escort for the doctrinal dance so that the worshiper can be transformed.[181] To do that well takes arduous preparation. The humility necessary for this is important because of the amount of time that is given to the sermon in the typical worship experience. It is the longest segment in the service.[182] In fact John Killinger has written that in the Puritan tradition of the religious awakenings in the early days of the United States it was not uncommon for preaching to last one and three quarters to two hours in length.[183] This reality should deeply affect the preacher. Who else receives that kind of attention? It's a heady thing and can go to the preacher's head. John Stott reminds us that while we are extolling the glories of Christ, we can, in reality, be seeking our own.[184] This should give us a holy pause.

Preaching in Worship

The preaching of the Scriptures is encompassed in the worship service. Rarely is the sermon first or last in the service. Other things lead into it and flow out of it. It is the main place where the preacher reminds the people of God of their redemptive story and gives the congregation a chance to *respond*.[185] That being said, it would seem to make sense to strive for pleasing continuity between the sermon and other elements in the service. The sermon interfaces with song, prayer, communion, offering, and even the body life of the church (maybe announcements can be spiritual). Whether or not the people discern the continuity or find the threads that weave themselves through the service, the preacher and the

---

180. This impressive Christian servant washed pots and pans to the glory of God.
181. Robert Smith, Jr. *Doctrine That Dances: Bringing Doctrinal Preaching and Teaching to Life* (Nashville: Broadman and Holman, 2008) 46.
182. Of course this varies from church to church. In Roman Catholic tradition the homily does not override the liturgy. In the Eastern Orthodox tradition the message is all but overpowered by the sights, sounds, and smells of worship. But in the evangelical (and even mainline Protestant denominations) the sermon is the longest segment of the service.
183. John Killinger, "Preaching and Worship," in *Handbook of Contemporary Preaching*, 432.
184. John Stott, *Between Two Worlds*, 321.
185. This is the main thrust of Dinelle Frankland's book, *His Story, Our Response: What the Bible Says about Worship* (Joplin, MO: College Press, 2008).

worship team probably need to be conscious of them. I told students for years that good preaching can take place even if the corporate expression of worship stinks. But it's always best if it's the other way. And sometimes, meaningful corporate worship has dug more than one sermon out of the homiletical ditch. In fact, sometimes great worshiping congregations can make a good preacher into a great one.

The above emphasis of coordinated worship has a strong history. In the Jewish synagogue certain texts were read on certain days (Luke 4:16-21). And a certain order seemed to have been preserved (Shema, prayers, blessings and curses, reading of the Law, reading of the Prophets, Benedictions, etc.). As the church marched across the Roman Empire this synagogue "order of service" seemed to follow her (Acts 2:42; 20:7-12). Finally, in ecclesiastical history there came the development of the "Christian Year." Few people in the free-church movement and nondenominational world are aware of it, but various Scripture readings were selected to be read within the calendar so that the gospel story could be read and appropriated during each calendar year.[186] To do this well, especially in a free-church tradition, takes hard work and aggressive planning.

> ...good preaching can take place even if the... worship stinks. But it's always best if it's the other way.

Part of preaching in worship deals with the actual reading of the sermon text in the service somewhere. In free-church traditions it is most common to read the sermon text within the sermon proper. This seems appropriate and probably gives the preacher some control over what he or she is going to do with the text. Sometimes the preacher wants to unpack the sermon text in sections so this method might be practically best. At other times the sermon text can be read outside of the sermon proper. It could be done prior to the actual delivery of the message.[187] It might be done in dramatic ways by other members of the worship team or drama ministry. Congregational reading of the text is also helpful at

---

186. I had an embarrassing moment in my early days of preaching ministry concerning this. I was attending a ministerial meeting of area ministers (pastors). Represented were ministers from my tradition as well as Catholics, Baptists, Methodists, and Lutherans. The discussion concerned having an ecumenical service during the Easter season instead of during the Thanksgiving season (which had been the custom). They suggested having a Maundy-Thursday service. I said, "Well, which day, Monday or Thursday?" They looked at me like I had lost my lectionary.

187. My father, a preacher of the gospel for almost sixty-eight years, liked the practice of reading his text prior to the message—sometimes prior to the special music (those were the days)—which preceded his sermon. His thinking was that people could be reflecting on that reading while the special music was taking place. Wishful thinking on his part?

times. Wherever the reading of the sermon text takes place, ponder these items:

1. Strive to ensure that there is a reverence for the reading of the text. I am not suggesting a *lifeless* reading of the text. Certain passages are pretty funny. But gaining everyone's attention through silence and a good clear public address system can help. It has always interested me that when the church is in corporate prayer you can hear a pin drop (we want God to hear us). But when God is addressing us in his Word people move around like a Wall Street Broker. What's wrong with this picture?

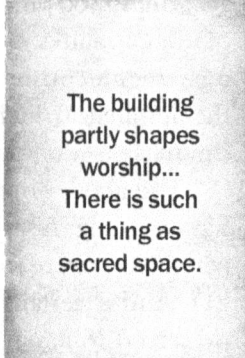

The building partly shapes worship... There is such a thing as sacred space.

2. Read the text well. The preacher (or whoever is assigned to read the text) does not have to read it like a British actor, but the reading should be done with excellence. This requires practice and care.

3. Remember that the reading of the text is the congregation's first exegesis of the text. The preacher has had all week (at least) studying the passage. He or she is familiar with the text's nuances. But for the congregation this is the first pass. This is an interpretive exercise.

4. Read the text deliberately. Don't rush it—even if the text is large.[188] Act like the congregation has all day for this. Maybe they should (see Neh 8:1-10). If we rush the reading of the text and then spend more time on *our* words, what conclusion will the congregation draw?

5. Read the text in company with the total life of the church in mind. Maybe the church observes a coordinated system of Bible reading and preaching. If people are joining Bible reading at home with what the church is preaching through at the time, judicious reading of the text can also take place in the service.

---

[188]. Large texts are a challenge. It takes some skill to read large passages in public and retain the attention. Practice helps. But one can economize in appropriate ways too. For instance I heard Marshall Leggett preach at Broadway Christian Church in Lexington, Kentucky, some years ago. His text was Acts 10:1–11:18, the gospel going to the Gentile world. That is a large and involved text. He chose to read publically just Acts 11:1-18. Wise choice. Acts 1:1-18 is a nice summation of everything that happened in Acts 10:1-48. A trick of the trade by a master preacher.

For years our family worshiped at the College Heights Christian Church in Joplin, Missouri. This congregation, from its earliest days, has preached expositorially through Bible books as part of its congregational life and rhythm. In the early days of the church everything came from the same place in the Bible for that Sunday. The Bible School classes all studied the same chapter from which the sermon came. In addition to that the communion meditation and the offering meditation also came from that same chapter or section. Sometimes getting everything from that section of Scripture was a bit of a hermeneutical stretch. But people learned a portion of God's Word that day, and the preacher could count on the people having read the text without necessarily reading it in the service.

Depending on one's church tradition, part of preaching in worship has to do with offering an invitation or decision time based on the preaching of the Word. Certainly in the United States we have gone way past the revivalist days of our Movement's birth. Altar calls, mourners' benches, and invitations are not priorities as they once were. (See chapter ten for JK's advice in concluding a sermon.) If the invitation appeal is attached to the sermon, make sure it is not divorced from the content of the text. Let the text win even in the invitational appeal. Beyond that my advice is fourfold:

> Read the text deliberately. Don't rush it—even if the text is large.

1. Be clear. This is not the place for heavy figurative language. Tell the people plainly what you want them to do.

2. Be concise. As JK mentioned, land the plane. Don't keep circling the airstrip thinking this will get better.

3. Be convicting. This is the last moment to do some *heart* work.

4. Be kind. There is no reason to alienate your audience at this point.[189] Remove obstacles for them to respond.

---

189. There are some glorious exceptions to this advice, especially in the Bible itself. The greatest sermon ever preached ends with a house built on a sand castle crashing against the rocks (Matt 57:24-27). And Paul's sign-off from his sermon in Antioch of Pisidia hardly qualifies as a walk in Mr. Roger's neighborhood (Acts 13:41). There is a time and place for such harsh appeals. But maybe they are the exceptions; not the rules. At times people need to know what to do to be saved (Acts 2:37; 16:30). We have the privilege of telling them kindly.

A final part of preaching in worship has to do with the preacher himself and the building in which the preaching takes place. This is so contextualized that it is difficult to say anything of substance that will have lasting value. The little poem says, "Methods are many; principles are few; methods always change, principles never do." That is true here.

> If the invitation appeal is attached to the sermon... Let the text win even in the invitational appeal.

When you raise issues about pulpit etiquette, the sky is the limit as to what is acceptable and what is not. Preachers must think like missionaries and do their best. Things like dress codes, ascending the stage, descending the stage, sitting on a stool and having a table close by, using a formal pulpit or a music stand, and the use of media are all issues of pulpit etiquette. Most of these cultural constraints have been long jettisoned in the free-church tradition in the West. It was good to see some of them go. The only rule these days seems to be, *communicate*. But be careful of throwing the baby out with the bath water. Scripture does call us to dress with modesty and do things decently and in order. There is something to be said for propriety and decorum. These can exist within what is viewed as real and authentic.

You could put what I know about church architecture in a thimble. Some preaching does take place in the open air, but most preaching takes place in a building of some kind.[190] This much I know:

> Architecture is theology. The building betrays faith understanding. Is the building a cathedral in the shape of a cross? Is the building a little storefront? Is the building a rented facility (bank, theater, mall)? In the building is the pulpit higher than the communion table or the other way around?

You make (i.e., build) the building, and then the building makes you. The building partly shapes worship once the congregation enters it. There is such a thing as sacred space. Think about that in relation to the preaching of the Word.[191] Few things are as impactful as when the

---

190. Church buildings didn't exist until the third and fourth century A.D. when Christianity was acceptable in the Roman Empire. Although there might be some evidence that there could have been a building in Jordan as early as A.D. 70.
191. While in Illinois in my first full-time ministry, the church built a new building. The committee decided to put in an expensive public address system. Some members complained about the

church gathers in the name of God to hear the preaching of the Word of God, to retell the story of the love of God, to confess their sins for the mercy of God, to commune and pray to achieve intimacy with God, to lift their voices in song to God, and to leave dumbfounded by the mystery of God as they go out to do his will in the world en route to the new creation of God.

---

dollars used. However the elders gave a good response. They said, "Look, the most important thing that happens in this building is the hearing of the Word of God. If people can't hear it, we won't accomplish our purpose as a church."

my thoughts higher than thoughts.

10 "For as the rain and the snow come down from heaven, and return not thither but water the earth, making it bring forth and sprout, giving seed to the sower and bread to the eater, shall my word be that goes forth from my mouth; it shall not return to me empty, it shall accomplish that which I purpose, and prosper in the thing for which I sent it.

u shall go out in joy, e led forth in peace; ntains and the hills before the reak forth into singing for m e trees of the field shall eir hands.
he thorn

CONCLUSION (JK)

A final word might feel a bit anticlimatic, but failing to conclude a conversation without some kind of farewell is simply rude. Mark and I want to thank you for entering into this extended talk with us. We are forever grateful for those of you who are committed to lifelong proclamation of the Word. We recognize that this preaching business takes place in a variety of settings and through an enormous collection of differing personalities. It also requires colossal diligence and discipline. Truth be told, all of us are rookies in this business of preaching. Each of us is an ongoing learner in the art and science of proclamation. I recently read Abraham Kuruvilla's challenging book, *Privilege the Text*. His work is a fresh reminder of the distance that exists between the ancient text and the contemporary listener. Dr. Kuruvilla's emphasis on the theology of the text is spot on and is a needed reminder of the urgency in reading, studying, living, and applying the Bible with a Christ-centered understanding. I am grateful for his encouragement.

> Truth be told, all of us are rookies in this business of preaching.

". . . The preaching of Scripture is not for the purpose of imparting information, but for transforming people by the power of the Holy Spirit—the changing of lives to conform to the image of Christ, by the instrumentality of God's Word. Week by week, sermon by sermon, pericope by pericope, habits are changed, dispositions are created, character is built, and the image of Christ is formed" (268).

> Our humble exhortation is simple. Preach on and let the text win.

Our humble exhortation is simple. Preach on and let the text win. May "the grace of the Lord Jesus Christ and the love of God and the fellowship of the Holy Spirit be with you all" as we await our King's return (2 Cor 13:14).

my thoughts than your thoughts.

10 "For as the rain and the snow come down from heaven, and return not thither but water the earth, making it bring forth and sprout, giving seed to the sower and bread to the eater, shall my word be that goes forth from my mouth; it shall not return to me empty, it shall accomplish that which I purpose, and prosper in the thing for which I sent it.

you shall go out in joy, and be led forth in peace; the mountains and the hills before you shall break forth into singing, and the trees of the field shall clap their hands.
Instead of the thorn sh

APPENDIX A
Tips for Letting the Text Win in a Postmodern World
DR. MARK SCOTT

NOTE: These twelve tips are not offered to dull the gospel or tame the text. They are merely presented so as to give the gospel the best chance to succeed in the current climate. Remember, they are more significant in the post-Christian West.

1. Be as global in your thinking as possible. Strive to keep any part of the message from being provincial or tribal.
2. Allow Acts 17 to help your introductions. Move inductively at first so as not to needlessly alienate your audience.
3. Agree with your opponents as far as possible. This will at least seem democratic to people. Be gracious in how you treat enemies of the faith. Pretend they are in the audience.
4. Anticipate their "contraries." Think like an unbeliever as you prepare.
5. Use asides and disclaimers when appropriate. This does not have to dull the gospel.
6. Distinguish effects of postmodernism and fads and trends in a postmodern culture.
7. Do not only declare the content of the gospel, but also model in life what it means to be a follower of Christ.
8. Gain a healthy interaction with books, media, and the culture of the current scene.
9. Strive to build a counterculture community that acts in love. Think of the gospel as an alternative narrative to what most people see around them.
10. Put love in your content and voice. Show people that you keep in mind their sensitivities and that you are sympathetic to their way of thinking. Confront the culture, but be humble. Have grace on tap.
11. Without being trendy or faddish use a contemporary idiom.
12. Assume very little. Your congregation is composed of "mixed nuts."

my thoughts than
thoughts.

10 "For as the rain and the snow c
down from heaven,
and return not thither but wa
the earth,
making it bring forth and sprou
giving seed to the sower and bread
to the eater,
so shall my word be that goes forth
from my mouth;
it shall not return to me empty,
but it shall accomplish that which
I purpose,
and prosper in the thing for which
I sent it.

"...u shall go out in joy,
..e led forth in peace;
...ntains and the hills before
...
...reak forth into singing,
...the trees of the field sha..
...eir hands.
...he thorn s...

APPENDIX B
How to Know If the Text is Winning
DR. MARK SCOTT

NOTE: How would we know if the text is winning? Here are some ways to know if the text is having its way and has the clout of the sermon.

Canonical Ways to Know:

1. Heartburn — Luke 24:27,32
2. Brokenness—conviction beyond what mortals can produce — Neh 8:9; Acts 3:27; Dan 9:2
3. Renewal—of faith and joy — Neh 8:17; Ps 1
4. Amazement and perceived authority — Matt 7:28-29; John 7:17
5. Faith engendered — Rom 10:17
6. Wisdom and power of God exposed—understanding beyond what mortals could know — 1 Cor 1:25
7. Baptism — Acts 8:34-38
8. Apathy and energy — Acts 13, 17
9. Specificity of life — Ps 19:7-11
10. Ambiguity — Rev 10:9
11. Anger — Luke 4:16-30; Acts 7

Non-Canonical Ways to Know:

1. Do they want to go home and reread the text? The Bonhoeffer test.
2. Does the text become a life marker, i.e., memorable? A life verse?
3. Do they make specific comment on some exegetical nugget?
4. Is there evidence of life change?
5. Does the evidence give evidence of the "lean in?"
6. What do people say about other preachers and their preaching?

my thoughts than
my thoughts.

10 "For as the rain and the snow come down from heaven,
and return not thither but water the earth,
making it bring forth and sprout,
giving seed to the sower and bread to the eater,
shall my word be that goes forth from my mouth;
it shall not return to me empty,
it shall accomplish that which I purpose,
and prosper in the thing for which I sent it.

u shall go out in joy,
e led forth in peace;
ntains and the hills before
reak forth into singing,
the trees of the field sha
eir hands.
he thorn sh

APPENDIX C
Preaching Schedule – 2013-14
Eastview Christian Church
Normal, IL

DR. J.K. JONES

"UNCHAINED: Dangerous Letters from a Prisoner of Rome"

(A study of seven Pauline epistles:
Ephesians, Philippians, Colossians, Philemon, 1 & 2 Timothy, Titus)

Title passage: 2 Timothy 2:8-9

Bam!
How Fearless Followers Become Super Heroes

These sermon texts are high impact Scriptures. Like the famous comic book expressions, these sermons are designed for an immediate punch to the soul spurring us on to spiritual growth. Each week we will challenge our congregation with teachings that call for immediate action and response!

Introductions (All books 1:1-2, Philemon 1-3, Titus 1:1-4) . . . . . July 7
In this sermon, we will look at the introduction of each of these letters Paul wrote. We will note the circumstance and background for these epistles as we explain how each was historically written as a *dangerous witness* of Paul. Though he was often chained, the gospel was not, as Paul mentions in his second letter to Timothy: "This is my gospel, for which I am suffering even to the point of being chained like a criminal. But God's word is not chained!"

Fight the Good Fight (1 Timothy 6:11-16) . . . . July 14
This sermon will encourage our people, young and old to approach their faith like a prize fighter from the first century. Here he encourages Timothy to fight by fleeing the things of the world, pursuing

righteousness, and taking hold of the good confession of Christ.

I Now Consider Loss (Philippians 3:7-11) .... July 21
These famous words from the letter to the Philippians will teach us that the way to gain Christ and all that comes with relationship with Him is to lose it all. Here Paul testifies that he has lost it all for the surpassing greatness of knowing Jesus. He has left a life of titles and accomplishment behind in order to experience the power of His resurrection.

Fan the Flame (2 Timothy 1:6 & 7) .... July 28
The teaching from this famous passage will encourage every Christian to use their spiritual gifts. We may not have had a prophecy over us telling us what our gift was, but the word promises and that each Christ-follower is filled with the Spirit and gifted by Him. Focusing on His gift in us gets us past our timidity and makes us fearless Christ-followers filled with power, love, and self-discipline.

I Kneel before the Father (Ephesians 3:14-21 – PRAY) ..... August 4
This sermon will focus on one of Paul's most famous prayers, the one he prays for the believers in the church at Ephesus. Learning from the apostle's example, we will understand that our prayers should focus on God strengthening us with His power and establishing us in His love. In this way we will grow to full maturity in Him.

Preach the Word (2 Timothy 4:1-5) – PREACH) .... August 11
In what was likely the last letter Paul ever wrote, he encouraged his son in the faith to keep preaching. According to the apostle this is the work of the evangelist and should be practiced always in the church for correcting, rebuking, and encouraging. We will celebrate the preaching of the word of God on this Sunday and talk about why it holds such a high priority for us.

I Have You in My Heart
(Philippians 1:3-11 – COMMUNITY) .... August 18
NOTE: VISION SUNDAY! – 25 minute vision/30 minute sermon
On this Sunday we will talk about how important the Christian community of faith is. The apostle thought fondly of this community in Philippi who were partners with him in the gospel, and we will

focus on our partnership in advancing the good news of Jesus in our world. This teaching will lend itself to a time of vision casting for our community of faith at Eastview.

He Has Served with Me (Philippians 2:19-30 – SERVE) . . . August 25
If we are to be the kind of Christ-followers Jesus desires, we must become servants like Him. In this teaching, Paul commends two great servants of the faith. Timothy is commended as one who serves, and Epaphroditus is called a fellow-worker. We will be challenged to serve like them.

Paul's Testimony (1 Timothy 1:12-17 – SHARE) . . . . September 1
In this passage we get a personal testimony from one of the greatest Christ followers ever. Paul unashamedly shares his story of conversion because of the grace and mercy of God on him. We will be encouraged to share what God has done in our lives so that He may receive "honor and glory forever and ever."

Charge It to Me (Philemon 17-22 – GIVE) . . . . September 8
On the day we intend to announce how we are going to generously give the surplus of our general fund budget away, we will examine the giving that Paul encourages in his letter to our first-century brother, Philemon. In a subtle way, the apostle encourages his friend to give up his ownership of his earthly slave and gain him as a Christian brother.

All over the World (Colossians 1:3-8 – GLOBAL) . . . . . September 15
We will end our "Bam" series with an encouragement to spread the good news to the world. Here the apostle tells the Colossian church that "all over the world this gospel is bearing fruit and growing" and that reality continues to this day. We will encourage our church to continue our desire to be a dangerous witness to the world.

OPEN
(An Invitation to Dangerous Witness)

This all-church study will be a six-week series accompanied by a book, study guide, and small group video lessons. We will encourage 4,000 Eastview members and attendees to be open to sharing their faith in the months following the series. Each sermon will reveal something that must open for the gospel of Jesus to be shared.

Open Lives (Philemon 4-7) . . . . September 22
This sermon will challenge Eastview Church to become people whose everyday lives are open to sharing their faith. In this passage, Paul commends Philemon for being active in sharing his faith by living it in his world and we will be encouraged to do the same.

Open Arms (Philippians 1:12-18). . . . . September 29
Even though Paul's arms literally have chains on them due to his imprisonment, they are open to anyone who will listen to his message. He is literally extending the gospel of Christ to anyone and everyone who will listen—even those who oppose him and are competing with him. We will be encouraged to embrace our situation in order to extend the grace of Jesus through open arms.

Open Witness (Philippians 2:14-18). October 6
This scripture encourages the people of first-century Philippi to live in such a way that they shine like stars in the universe. If we are to make a difference in our world, we will have to live godly lives and hold out the word or truth in this dark world we live in. The day of Christ is coming, so we like Paul, run, labor, and pour ourselves out for the gospel message.

Open to All (Colossians 1:28 & 29) . . . . October 13
The thing that Paul labors for, according to this teaching, is to proclaim Jesus to everyone. In this sermon we will encourage our congregation to see everyone as potential believers and to rely on God's power working in them to share their faith.

Open Mouth (Ephesians 6:19-20) . . . . October 20
Paul's prayer at the end of his letter to Ephesus is that God will help when he opens his mouth. Our goal in this sermon will be continued encouragement to fearlessly open our mouths to make known the "good news" of Jesus.

APPENDIX C

Open Doors (Colossians 4:2-6)–(Ajai Lall) . . . . October 27
This Sunday will conclude our series with our partner, Ajai Lall bringing the message. Through this passage in Colossians and stories of ministry in India, he will encourage us to see prayer as the key to evangelizing those who are lost. Our prayer, along with Paul, is that God will open doors for the message, help us proclaim the message, and give us wisdom for how to make the most of every opportunity.

(Made)

The title of this sermon series is from the MTV show "Made" where teenagers were followed as they transformed into the people they dreamed about being. Playing off of Jesus' command to go and "make disciples," this series will look at four teachings on spiritual formation and how we are "made" to be more like Jesus as we follow Him.

Epaphras' Prayer (Colossians 4:12) . . . . November 3
In this verse we find that one of Paul's ministry partners was committed to the Colossian church with a consistent prayer. Epaphras was praying for these loved disciples to mature and stand firm and will become the foundation for our series of becoming the disciples Jesus wants us to be as we cooperate with the Holy Spirit's work in us.

Not Swayed & Equipped (Ephesians 4:10-16) . . . . November 10
This teaching on discipleship will focus on the role each individual member has in the body of Christ as we equip each other as different body parts with different gifts. Being made into disciples requires involvement in the church. We do not mature alone.

Rooted & Established (Colossians 2:6 & 7) . . . . November 17
Jesus teaches in John 15 that if we are to bear fruit for Him, we must remain in Him, the truth vine. In this passage the apostle confirms this reality, reminding us that as we continue to live in Christ, we will be strengthened in our faith. To be made like Christ is to be rooted in Him.

Press On (Philippians 3:12-15) . . . . November 24
This final teaching on the disciple-making life encourages us to keep going. In this famous passage, Paul says there is "one thing" he does. He forgets the past and strains toward what lies ahead. Part of spiritual formation comes from a life of perseverance as we press toward our heavenly goal.

Christ "mas"
This Christmas season series will focus on major Christ passages as we celebrate the birth of Jesus into the world. Using the Spanish word for "more" (as in "live mas" of the Taco Bell advertisements) we will inject "more" Jesus into the Christmas season with these important teachings about who this baby born in Bethlehem really is.

Supremacy of Christ (Colossians 1:15-20) . . . . December 1
Jesus was born as a baby in a manger, but He is so much more than a cuddly Christmas story. He is in fact the "everything" of the universe. In this teaching we will proclaim along with the apostle that Jesus is God, that He created all things, that He holds it all together, and that He reconciled all things to God.

Christ's Attitude (Philippians 2:5-11) . . . . December 8
If the Christmas story in Luke 2 is the human view of the birth of the Christ child, then this passage is the heavenly/cosmic view. What happened when God became flesh and was born of a virgin? Christ chose to take the form of a servant and gave His life on the cross. In this season of gift-giving we will learn that our attitude should be like Christ's when it comes to generosity.

In Christ (Ephesians 1:3-14) . . . . December 15
This teaching will show us all that God intended for us and all that we are "in Christ." It is this "in Christ" condition that helps us find belonging and purpose in this season when so many struggle to find it in the things of this world. The story of Christmas is that we were included in Christ by believing in this salvation gospel.

Christ the Savior Appeared (Titus 3:3-7) . . . . December 22
As Paul writes to his preaching apprentice Titus, in chapter three he

reminds him of how foolish, enslaved, and hateful this world was, and then he gives the true meaning of the Christmas story: "when the kindness and love of God our Savior appeared, he saved us. . . ." Merry Christmas!

Mystery of Christ Made Known (Colossians 1:24-27). . . December 29
With the Christmas holidays behind us we still have one more lesson concerning the continuing gift of Christmas. The glorious riches of this precious gift Jesus is a mystery that is literally living in us. By following Him, we live out the hope of glory in our lives and in our witness.

2014

"KEY" CHAIN VERSES

(Idea, key chain for each verse, or dog tags with each verse to put on a key chain. This is a play on the words "Key" – important, and "Chain" – letters written in chains. Double entendré.)

2 Timothy 3:16 – "All Scripture is God breathed" . . . . January 5

Ephesians 2:8-10 – "For it is by grace you have been saved" January 12

Philippians 1:21 – "To live is Christ to die is gain" . . . . January 19

Colossians 3:17 – "Do it all in the name of The Lord" . . . . January 26

1 Timothy 4:12 – "Set an example . . ." . . . . February 2

Titus 3:14 – "Do what is good" . . . . February 9

Philemon 6 – "Active in sharing your faith" . . . . February 16

Family series/household/relationships

Eph. 5:25-31; Col. 3:18-19 – "Husbands, love your wife" . . February 23

Ephesians 5:22-24 – "Wives, submit to your husband" . . . . March 2

Ephesians 6:1-3; Col. 3:20 – "Children, obey your parents" . . March 9

Ephesians 6:4; Col. 3:21 – "Nurture your children" . . . . March 16

Ephesians 6:5-9; Col. 3:22–4:2 –
"Slaves obey your masters" . . . . March 23

1 Timothy 5:1 & 2, Titus 2:1-8 – Generations . . . . March 30

1 Timothy 5:3-16 – Widows . . . . April 6

Philippians 4:2 & 3 – "Get along" . . . . April 13

1 Timothy 3:16 – The gospel in one verse (EASTER) . . . . April 20

CHURCH: THE HOPE OF THE WORLD

Col. 1:13; Phil. 3:20; 2 Tim. 4:18; Eph. 2:9 – Citizenship . . . . . April 27

Ephesians 2:14-22 – Built Together . . . . May 4

Ephesians 3:7-12 – Through the Church . . . . May 11

Ephesians 4:1-6 – ONE . . . . May 18

1 Timothy 3:14 & 15 – Church of the Living God . . . . May 25

NOT YOUR FAVORITE SCRIPTURES
(or sermons you don't like, harsh words from the Word, etc.)

1 Timothy 2:9-15 – "A woman should learn in quietness" . . . . June 1

1 Timothy 1:18-20; Titus 3:9-10 – "handed over to Satan" . . . . June 8

1 Timothy 6:6-10,17-19 – "rich fall into a trap" . . . . June 15

Ephesians 5:3-7; 1 Timothy 1:8-11 –
"God's wrath on disobedient" . . . . June 22

Philippians 1:15-18 – "preach Christ out of selfish ambition" June 29

APPENDIX C

CHURCH LEADERSHIP

Colossians 2:8,18,22; 1 Timothy 1:3; 6:3; Phil. 1:10 –
"Leadership: Why? #1 – Counter Bad Influences"............ July 6

Titus 1:5-15 – "Leadership: Why? #2 –
Leaders in Each church"................................. July 13

1 Timothy 3:1-7 – "Who? – Traits of a Leader".............. July 20

1 Timothy 3:8-13 – "Who else? – Servant Leaders" .... July 27

1 Timothy 5:17-18 – "Respect for Genuine Leadership".... August 3

HONORABLE MENTIONS

Colossians 4:10-18 – Aristarchus, Mark, Jesus, and Luke... August 10

Ephesians 6:21; Colossians 4:7; 1 Timothy 4:12;
Titus 3:12 – Tychicus .... August 17

Colossians 4:14; 2 Timothy 4:10; Philemon 24 –
NOT Demas .... August 24

Colossians 4:9; Philemon 10 – Onesimus .... August 31

2 Timothy 4:9-21 – "The List" .... September 7

my thoughts than my thoughts.

10 "For as the rain and the snow come down from heaven, and return not thither but water the earth, making it bring forth and sprout, giving seed to the sower and bread to the eater, shall my word be that goes forth from my mouth; it shall not return to me empty, it shall accomplish that which I purpose, and prosper in the thing for which I sent it.

you shall go out in joy, and be led forth in peace; the mountains and the hills before you shall break forth into singing, and the trees of the field shall clap their hands. the thorn

WORKS CITED

Allen, Ronald J. *Contemporary Biblical Interpretation for Preaching*. Valley Forge, PA: Judson, 1974.

Allison, Lon. "God the Evangelist." In *Preaching Today*. Cassette Tape #210.

Aristotle. *The Rhetoric*. Pearson, 1960.

Arthurs, Jeffrey D. *Preaching with Variety: How to Re-create the Dynamics of Bible Genres*. Grand Rapids: Kregel, 2007.

Bailey, E.K. "Brevity in Preaching." In *Leadership*, Fall, 1997.

Bailey, Raymond. *Paul the Preacher*. Nashville: Broadman Press, 1991.

Barna, George. *Leaders on Leadership*. Ventura, CA: Regal Books, 1997.

Barth, Karl. *Dogmatics in Outline*. New York: Harper Torch Books, 1959.

Begg, Alistair. *Preaching for God's Glory*. Wheaton, IL: Crossway Books, 1999.

Beitzel, Barry. *The Moody Atlas of Bible Lands*. Chicago: Moody, 1985.

Benson, Bob. *See You at The House*. Nashville: Generoux Nelson, 1989.

Blackwood, Andrew. *The Preparation of Sermons*. New York: Abingdon, 1948.

Block, Daniel. "Christian Living and Teaching of Old Testament Law." Professional Growth Seminar. Sponsored by *Ministry Magazine*, April, 2005.

Blomberg, Craig. *Interpreting the Parables*. Downers Grove, IL: InterVarsity, 1990.

Bray, Gerald. *Biblical Interpretation: Past and Present*. Downers Grove, IL: InterVarsity, 1996.

Broadus, John A. *On the Preparation and Delivery of Sermons*. Rev. by Vernon Stanfield. San Francisco: Harper and Row, 1979.

Brown, Stephen. "Illustrating the Sermon" in *Handbook of Contemporary Preaching*. Ed. by Michael Duduit. Nashville: Broadman, 1993.

Brueggemann, Walter. *Finally Comes the Poet: Daring Speech for Proclamation.* Minneapolis: Fortress, 1989.

Bryson, Harold T. *Expository Preaching: The Art of Preaching through a Bible Book.* Nashville: Broadman & Holman, 1999.

Buttrick, David. *Homiletic: Moves and Structures.* Philadelphia: Fortress, 1987.

Caird, G.B. *The Language and Imagery of the Bible.* London: Duckworth, 1980.

Carson, Donald, ed. *Worship by the Book.* Grand Rapids: Zondervan, 2002.

Carter, Terry G., J. Scott Duval, and J. Daniel Hays. *Preaching God's Word.* Grand Rapids: Zondervan, 2005.

Chappell, Bryan. *Christ Centered Preaching: Redeeming the Expository Sermon.* Grand Rapids: Baker, 1994.

_____. "The Future of Expository Preaching. In *Preaching Magazine.* September–October, 2004.

Cotterell, Peter, and Max Turner. *Linguistics and Biblical Interpretation.* Downers Grove, IL: InterVarsity, 1989.

Craddock, Fred. *As One Without Authority.* Nashville: Abingdon, 1971.

_____. *Preaching.* Nashville: Abingdon, 1985.

Dargan, Edwin C. *A History of Preaching.* 2 vol. Repr. Grand Rapids: Baker, 1968.

Davis, H. Grady. *Design for Preaching.* Philadelphia: Fortress, 1958.

Dodd, C.H. *The Apostolic Preaching and Its Development.* Grand Rapids: Baker, 1980.

Doty, William. *Letters in Primitive Christianity.* Philadelphia: Fortress, 1973.

Duduit, Michael, ed. *Handbook of Contemporary Preaching.* Nashville: Broadman, 1993.

_____. *Preaching Truth in a Whatever World.* Conference Attended by JK and Dr. Chuck Sackett. Sponsored by Total Living Network, Chicago, IL. November 17, 2004.

Eclov, Lee. "What Makes a Sermon Deep? The Sources of Wisdom Preaching." In *The Art and Craft of Biblical Preaching.* Ed. by Haddon Robinson and Craig Brian Larson. Grand Rapids: Zondervan, 2005.

Enyart, David. "Inductive Proclamation: The Question, the Quest, and the Discovery." In *Preaching through Tears.* Lincoln, IL: Lincoln Christian College and Seminary Alumni Association, 2000.

Evans, Tony. "Building on the Right Foundation." In *Preaching Today.* Cassette Tape #264.

Fant, Clyde. *Preaching for Today.* New York: Harper and Row, 1975.

Fant, Clyde E., and William M. Pinson, *20 Centuries of Great Preaching.* 13 Vol. Waco, TX: Word, 1971.

Fee, Gordon. *New Testament Exegesis: A Handbook for Students and* Pastors. Philadelphia: Westminster, 1983.

Fee, Gordon, and Douglas Stuart. *How to Read the Bible for All Its Worth: A Guide to Understanding the Bible* (Second Edition). Grand Rapids: Zondervan, 1993.

Fitch, Alger. *What the Bible Says about Preaching.* Joplin, MO: College Press, 1989.

Foster, Richard. *Celebration of Discipline.* San Francisco: Harper and Row, 1978.

Frankland, Dinelle. *His Story, Our Response: What the Bible Says about Worship.* Joplin, MO: College Press, 2008.

Fuller, David Otis, ed. *Spurgeon's Lectures to His* Students. Grand Rapids: Zondervan, 1955.

Gabel, John B., and Charles B. Wheeler. *The Bible as Literature: An Introduction,* 2nd ed. New York: Oxford University Press, 1986.

Galli, Mark, and Craig Larson. *Preaching That Connects.* Grand Rapids: Zondervan, 1994.

Gibson, Scott, ed. *Preaching to a Shifting Culture.* Grand Rapids: Baker Books, 2004.

_____. *Should We Use Someone Else's Sermon?* Grand Rapids: Zondervan, 2008.

Godawa, Brian. *Word Pictures: Knowing God through Story and Imagination.* Downers Grove, IL: InterVarsity, 2009.

Goldsworthy, Graeme. *Preaching the Whole Bible as Christian Scripture.* Grand Rapids: Eerdmans, 2000.

Greidanus, Sidney. *The Modern Preacher and the Ancient Text.* Grand Rapids: Eerdmans, 1986.

_____. *Preaching Christ from the Old Testament.* Grand Rapids: Eerdmans, 1999.

Grenz, Stanley J.A. *A Primer on Postmodernism.* Grand Rapids: Eerdmans, 1996.

Guinness, Os. "The Humiliation of the Word." In *Fit Bodies, Fat Minds: Why Evangelicals Don't Think and What to Do about It.* Grand Rapids: Baker, 1994.

Hamilton, J. Wallace. *Still the Trumpet Sounds.* Old Tappan, NJ: Fleming H. Revell, 1970.

Havner, Vance. *Pepper 'n' Salt.* Grand Rapids: Baker, 1983.

Henderson, David C. *Culture Shift: Connecting God's Truth to our Changing World.* Grand Rapids: Baker, 1998.

Jakes, T.D. *Preaching.* September–October, 2003.

Johnson, Darrell W. *The Glory of Preaching: Participating in God's Transformation of the World.* Downers Grove, IL: InterVarsity, 2009.

Johnston, Graham. *Preaching to a Postmodern World: A Guide to Reaching Twenty-First Century Listeners.* Grand Rapids: Baker, 2001.

Jones, JK. *Reading with God in Mind.* Joplin, MO: HeartSpring, 2004.

Jowett, J.H. *The Preacher: His Life and Work.* London: Forgotten Books, 2012.

Kaiser, Walter. *Preaching and Teaching from the Old Testament.* Grand Rapids: Baker, 2003.

Kaiser, Walter, and Moises Silva. *An Introduction to Biblical Hermeneutics: The Search for Meaning.* Grand Rapids: Zondervan, 1994.

Keyer, Jonathan, ed. *Great Preaching.* Nashville: The Preaching Library, 2002.

Killinger, John. *Fundamentals of Preaching.* Philadelphia: Fortress, 1985.

_____. "Preaching and Worship." In *Handbook of Contemporary Preaching.* Ed. by Michael Duduit. Nashville: Broadman, 1992.

King, Darrel. *Men of Faith: E.M. Bounds.* Minneapolis: Bethany House, 1998.

Klein, William W., Craig L. Blomberg, and Robert L. Hubbard Jr. *Introduction to Biblical Interpretation.* Dallas: Word, 1993.

Koller, Charles W. *Expository Preaching Without Notes.* Grand Rapids: Baker, 1962.

Kuhn, Thomas. *The Structure of Scientific Revolutions.* Chicago: University of Chicago Press, 1996 repr.

Kuruvilla, Abraham. *Privilege the Text!* Chicago: Moody, 2013.

Lakoff, George, and Mark Johnson, *Metaphors We Live By.* Chicago: University of Chicago Press, 1980.

Lederer, Richard. *The Play of Words.* New York: Simon and Schuster, 1990.

Lewis, Ralph L., and Greg Lewis. *Inductive Preaching: Helping People Listen.* Westchester, IL: Crossway Books, 1983.

Liefeld, Walter, L. *New Testament Exposition.* Grand Rapids: Zondervan, 1984.

Lischer, Richard, ed. *The Company of Preachers: Wisdom on Preaching, Augustine to the Present.* Grand Rapids: Eerdmans, 2002.

Lose, David. *Confessing Jesus Christ: Preaching in a Postmodern World.* Grand Rapids: Eerdmans, 2003.

Lowry, Eugene. *The Homiletical Plot.* Atlanta: John Knox, 1980.

Lucas, Dick. "Preaching the Melody Line of the Text." *Preaching Today,* Cassette Tape # 239.

Lybrand, Fred. *Preaching on Your Feet.* Nashville: Broadman & Holman, 2008.

Lyotard, Jean-Francis. "The Postmodern Culture: A Report on Knowledge," *Theory of Knowledge.* Minneapolis: University of Minnesota, 1984.

MacArthur, John Jr. *Rediscovering Expository Preaching*. Dallas: Word, 1992.

McCartney, Dan, and Charles Clayton. *Let the Reader Understand: A Guide to Interpreting and Applying the Bible*. Wheaton, IL: Bridgepoint Books, 1994.

McLuhan, Marshall. *Understanding Media: The Extensions of Man*. New York: Signet Books, 1964.

Metzger, Bruce. *A Textual Commentary on the Greek New Testament*, 2nd ed. New York: American Bible Society, 1994.

Michelsen, A. Berkeley. *Interpreting the Bible*. Grand Rapids: Eerdmans, 1963.

Miller, Calvin. *Marketplace Preaching*. Grand Rapids: Baker, 1995.

_____. *Spirit, Word, and Story: A Philosophy of Preaching*. Dallas: Word, 1989.

Mohler, R. Albert Jr. *He Is Not Silent: Preaching in a Postmodern World*. Chicago: Moody, 2008.

Oldenburg, Ray. *The Great Good Place*. New York: Marlowe and Company, 1999.

Olford, Stephen F., and David L. Olford. *Anointed Expository Preaching*. Nashville: Broadman & Holman, 1998.

Ortberg, Nancy. "Modern Golden Calves." *Preaching Today*, Cassette Tape #203.

Pascal, Blaise. *The Mind on Fire*. Ed. by James M. Houston. In Victors Classics. Colorado Springs: David C. Cook, 2006.

Patzia, Arthur G., and Anthony J. Petrotta. *Pocket Dictionary of Biblical Studies*. Downers Grove, IL: InterVarsity, 2002.

Peterson, Eugene. *Tell It Slant*. Grand Rapids: Eerdmans, 2008.

Pitt-Watson, Ian. *A Primer for Preachers*. Grand Rapids: Baker, 1999.

Richards, E. Randolph. *First-Century Letter Writing: Secretaries, Composition, and Collection*. Downers Grove, IL: InterVarsity, 2004.

Robinson, Haddon. *Biblical Preaching: The Development and Delivery of Expository Messages*. Grand Rapids: Baker, 1980.

WORKS CITED

_____. *Making a Difference in Preaching.* Grand Rapids: Baker, 1999.

Robinson, Haddon, and Craig Brian Larson, eds. *The Art and Craft of Biblical Preaching.* Grand Rapids: Zondervan, 2005.

Ryken, Leland, James C. Wilhoit, and Tremper Longman III. *Dictionary of Biblical Imagery.* Downers Grove, IL: InterVarsity, 1998.

Schmutzer, Andrew J. "Using Biblical Hebrew in Sermon Preparation." In *The Moody Handbook of Preaching.* Ed. by John Koessler. Chicago: Moody, 2008.

Shakespeare, William. *The Tempest* in the Folger Shakespeare Library. Ed. by Barbara Mowat and Paul Werstine. New York: Simon and Schuster, 2004.

Shields, Bruce. *From the Housetops.* St. Louis: Chalice, 2000.

Skinner, Craig. "Creativity in Preaching." In *Handbook of Contemporary Preaching.* Ed. by Michael Duduit. Nashville: Broadman, 1992.

Smith, Robert Jr. *Doctrine That Dances: Bringing Doctrinal Preaching and Teaching to Life.* Nashville: Broadman & Holman, 2008.

Stanley, Andy, and Lane Jones. *Communicating for a Change.* Sisters, OR: Multnomah, 2006.

Stott, John R. W. *Between Two Worlds.* Grand Rapids: Eerdmans, 1982.

_____. "The Greatest Invitation Ever Made," *Preaching Today,* Cassette Tape # 277.

Taylor, Myron. "Trust the Word," *The Christian Standard.* 4 December 1977.

Turnbull, Ralph G. *A History of Preaching.* Vol. 3. Grand Rapids: Baker, 1974.

Van Harn, Roger. "The Preacher as Listener." *Preaching Magazine,* Jan-Feb, 1993.

Vanhoozer, Kevin J. ed. *The Cambridge Companion to Postmodern Theology* (Cambridge: Cambridge University Press, 2003).

Vines, Jerry. *A Practical Guide to Sermon Preparation.* Chicago: Moody, 1985.

Vines, Jerry, and James L. Shaddix. *Power in the Pulpit*. Chicago: Moody, 1999.

Webb, John D., and Joseph C. Grana II, eds. *Preaching through Tears*. Lincoln, IL: Lincoln Christian College and Seminary Alumni Association, 2000.

Webber, Frederick Roth. *A History of Preaching in Britain and America*, 3 vol. Northwestern, 1957.

Whitney, Donald. *Spiritual Disciplines for the Christian Life*. Colorado Springs: NavPress, 1991.

Wiersbe, Warren. "Imagination: The Preacher's Neglected Ally." In *The Art and Craft of Biblical Preaching: A Comprehensive Resource for Today's Communication*. Ed. by Haddon Robinson and Craig B. Larson. Grand Rapids: Zondervan, 2005.

Wiersbe, Warren, and Lloyd M. Perry. *The Wycliffe Handbook of Preaching and Preachers*. Chicago: Moody, 1984.

Wiersbe, Warren, and David Wiersbe. *The Elements of Preaching*. Carol Stream, IL: Tyndale House, 1986.

Williams, Paul. "And So It Goes." In *Christian Standard*. December 9, 2009.

Willimon, William, and Richard Lischer. *Concise Encylopedia of Preaching*. Louisville, KY: Westminster John Knox, 1995.

Wilson, Paul Scott. *A Concise History of Preaching*. Nashville: Abingdon, 1992.

Zuck, Roy. *Basic Bible Interpretation: A Practical Guide to Discovering Biblical Truth*. Wheaton, IL: Victor Books, 1991.

www.ingramcontent.com/pod-product-compliance
Lightning Source LLC
Chambersburg PA
CBHW071742150426
43191CB00010B/1659